AXIS

OF

HORIZON

인사말

국립현대미술관은 올해의 첫 전시로 《수평의 축》전을 개최합니다.
이번 전시는 국립현대미술관이 최근까지 수집한 국제미술 소장품을 가운데
'자연'을 주제로 구성한 기획전입니다. 미술관의 소장품은 그 미술관의
정체성을 보여주고 역사적 가치와 의미, 그리고 미래의 비전을 보여줍니다.

이번 전시에서 다루는 '자연'이라는 친숙한 주제는 '이웃집 같은
친근한 미술관, 개방적인 미술관'을 표방하는 국립현대미술관의 지향점과 잘
부합된다고 믿습니다. 이에 폭 넓은 관람객과 교감하고 예술적 영감을 공유할
수 있기를 기대합니다. 근대기에 이르러 미술의 주된 대상으로 자리 잡은 자연에
대한 탐구는 오늘날까지 지속적으로 확장되고 변화하고 있습니다.

《수평의 축》전시는 17명의 현대미술 작가들이 동시대적인 관점으로
바라보고 재해석하는 자연과 관련된 작품들로 구성되었습니다. 회화, 조각,
사진, 영상 등 다양한 매체의 작품들은 인간과 자연 사이의 오랜 길항관계와
자연의 요소와 현상에 대한 미적 실험, 나아가 사회·역사적인 내용을 포괄적으로
보여줍니다. 이번 전시를 통해 코로나19 상황 속에서 예술로 치유와 위로를
받고, 새로운 희망과 담론을 발견할 수 있기를 바랍니다.

이번 전시를 위해 애써주신 미술관 가족들에게 고마움을 전하며
모두가 예상치 못한 어려운 상황 속에서 작품대여를 허락하고 지원을 아끼지
않은 삼성미술관 리움, 국제갤러리, 리만 머핀 갤러리 등 소장처와 테레시타
페르난데즈, 제니퍼 스타인캠프, 바이런 킴, 김세진 등 참여 작가분들께
감사드립니다. 그리고 세계적인 수준의 소장품을 구입할 수 있도록
후원해주신 국립현대미술관 발전 후원위원회(MDC, 회장 윤석민)에도
깊은 감사의 말씀을 드립니다.

국립현대미술관장
윤범모

FOREWORD

The National Museum of Modern and Contemporary Art (MMCA) presents *Axis of Horizon* as its first exhibition of this year. This special exhibition consists of nature-themed works from among the international art acquired by MMCA through recent years. MMCA's collection is an illustration of its identity as a museum as well as its historical value, significance, and future vision.

I see the theme of "nature" in this exhibition as being well suited to MMCA's orientation as an institution, with its aims of becoming an "open museum that is as friendly as a neighbor's home." In that sense, I look forward to being able to connect with visitors and share artistic inspiration. All the way through to the modern era, explorations of nature have established themselves as a prominent subject of art, one that continues to grow and change even to this day.

The *Axis of Horizon* exhibition consists of works of art related to nature as seen and reinterpreted by 17 artists from a contemporary perspective. Encompassing a broad range of media from painting to sculpture, photography, and video, the works offer a comprehensive glimpse of the longstanding rivalry between humanity and nature, aesthetic experiments with natural elements and phenomena, and social and historical content. I also look forward to the exhibition providing a means of achieving healing and comfort through art amid the COVID-19 situation and discovering new hope and discourses.

I wish to express my thanks to the members of the MMCA curatorial team for all their efforts toward this exhibition; to Leeum, Samsung Museum of Art, Kukje Gallery, Lehmann Maupin Gallery, and the other institutions for their generous support and permission to borrow their work during these unexpected and difficult circumstances; and to the participating artists, including Teresita Fernández, Jennifer Steinkamp, Byron Kim, Kim Sejin, and many more. I would also like to share my deepest gratitude to the MMCA Director's Council (MDC, chairperson Sukmynn Yoon) for its support toward the acquisition of world-class works of art.

Youn Bummo
Director, National Museum of Modern and Contemporary Art, Korea

수평의 축

양옥금 국립현대미술관 학예연구사

《수평의 축》전은 국립현대미술관의 국제미술 소장품을 중심으로 구성된 기획전시이다. 이 전시는 르네상스 이후 근대로 이행하면서 오랫동안 탐색되고 예술적 재현을 시도해 온 전통적인 소재이자 주제인 '자연'을 동시대적 관점에서 재해석하고 다양한 형태로 조명하고자 기획되었다.

서양미술사에서 종교와 인간중심의 사고(思考)에서 파생된 주제들에 가려져 있던 '자연'은 17세기에 이르러서야 풍경화라는 독자적인 장르가 확립되면서 예술가들에 의해 적극적으로 다뤄지게 되었다. 또한 프랑수와 줄리앙(François Jullien)이 언급한 것처럼 "풍경이라는 용어가 회화의 진보 속에서 태어났다고는 하지만, 사실 풍경은 오랫동안 그림에서 배경이나 장식 역할만 하며 작품의 '빈 구석'을 채워 왔다. 이후 '역사'의 헤게모니로부터 벗어나면서, 다시 말해 신체를 통해 표현된 이상적인 미의 구속에서 벗어나면서, 그리고 '행위'의 의미를 따지는 일로부터도 자유로워지면서, 풍경은 유럽 예술의 중심부에 아주 천천히 자리를 잡아가게 되었다."[1] 《수평의 축》전은 자연을 처음으로 주체적인 미술의 대상으로 삼았던 풍경회화 이후 지속적으로 변화해 온 자연에 대한 접근방식을 보여준다. 이것은 현대미술의 미학적인 실험을 거쳐 생성되는 재해석을 바탕으로 한 자연에 대한 탐구뿐만 아니라 자연과 인간의 관계, 사회와 개인 그리고 역사를 포괄적으로 다룬다.

전통적으로 동양적 자연관이 인위적인 힘이 가해지지 않은 상태의 자연을 추구했다면, 서양의 자연관에서는 자연을 하나의 정복의 대상으로 간주했다.[2] 우리가 일반적으로 말하는 '풍경' 또한 자연을 개척하거나 다양한 방식의 문명적 상태로 변환한 풍경을 의미한다. 원초적이며 이상적인 자연을

의미하는 아르카디아(Arcadia)라는 개념이 유럽의 오랜 역사에 존재하지만 그것 역시 인간의 이상(理想)을 중심에 둔 자연관에서 생겨난 아름답고, 풍요로운 유토피아일 뿐이다. 이 전시에서는 자연에 대한 미적 탐구와 기록에서 비롯한 보이는 것들의 이면에 존재하는 다양한 층위를 살펴보고자 한다. 이는 문화적, 역사적 맥락에서 해석될 수 있는 풍경이 함축하는 과거와 현재를 교차시키는가 하면 자연과 인간의 공생을 환기시키고, 때로 자연의 현상과 비가시적인 요소 자체가 하나의 작품으로 시각화되거나 재해석되는 다양하고 다각적인 차원에서의 접근을 보여준다.

'수평의 축'이라는 전시 제목은 하늘이 대지 혹은 수면과 맞닿는 수평적 접점을 자연으로 상정하고 이에 대한 우리의 다양한 인식의 좌표를 그려볼 수 있는 축(axis) 세우기를 시도하는 것을 의미한다. 자연의 상징으로 상정한 '수평'은 '지평선을 풍경의 경계선'[3]으로 여겨왔던 개념과 연결 지을 수 있다. 여기에서 '축(axis)'은 자연을 다른 차원으로 바라보게 하는 창이자 문지방(threshold)과 같은 접점에 존재하며 자연의 내부와 외부, 인간과 문명의 경계를 유연하게 넘나드는 새로운 관점을 제안한다.

이번 전시는 회화와 조각 등 전통적인 매체부터 사진, 영상, 설치까지 아우르는 다양한 미디어 작품들로 자연에 대한 미학적 탐구와 오랜 역사를 통해 형성된 인간과 자연의 길항관계를 보여준다. 더하여 자연의 묘사와 재현, 삶에 대한 사유, 그리고 인간도 자연의 일부라는 자각을 일깨우면서 동시대 미술이 함의하는 메시지를 통해 현재에 대한 반성과 미래에 대한 모색을 꾀한다.

부분의 전체

'부분'이라는 것은 필연적으로 '전체'라는 개념에 종속성을 가진다. 부분은 하나이자 별개로 존재함으로써 그 자체로 전체가 되며, 전체의 일부로 작동하는 각각의 부분이 합쳐졌을 때 커다란 전체를 이루기도 한다. 전시의 도입부가 되는 〈부분의 전체〉는 자연의 단편적 재현을 통해 삶 자체에 대한 통찰을 다루는 작품들로 구성된다. 자연의 일부로서 인간의 한계와 공생을 보여주는 작품들은 역사와 현재, 그리고 미래에 대한 자각을 일깨운다. 이것은 자연의 제유(提喩)를 통해 근원적인 질문으로 다가서는 방법들을 보여주는 것이라고 할 수 있다.

제니퍼 스타인캠프는 컴퓨터 애니매이션과 영상 미디어를 이용하여 건축적인 공간과 움직임, 그리고 현상학적 인식을 새롭게 실험하는 작품들을 지속해 왔다. 특히 자연적인 요소에서 출발한 추상적 형태의 유기적 움직임을 3D 애니메이션으로 구현한 영상을 특정 공간에 투사하여 실재하는 공간과 환영 사이의 경계가 모호해지는 현상학적 인지 변화에 주목한다. 〈정물 3〉(2019)은 작가가 2016년부터 작업해 온 〈정물〉 연작 시리즈의 최근작 중 하나이다. 작가는 과일과 꽃은 정물화로 그려야 한다는 특히 16세기 네덜란드와 플랑드르 화가들의 바니타스 회화가 지닌 정적인 가치와 삶의 유한함을 은유했던 오랜 관습을 깨고자 했다. 이를 위해 정물화 속에 존재할 법한 과일과

꽃들을 가상의 공간에 채워 떠다니게 하고 충돌하게 하면서 삶과 자연의 생명이 지닌 에너지를 환기시킨다.

에이샤-리사 아틸라는 핀란드의 대표적인 시각예술가이자 영화제작자로 무빙 이미지를 이용한 영상설치와 영화, 사진, 드로잉 등의 폭 넓은 작업을 보여주고 있다. 초기에 작가는 미술이론, 제도비평, 페미니즘에서 출발한 개념미술 작업에 집중하였으나 1990년 이후부터는 이미지, 언어, 서사, 공간의 구축에 관심을 가지고 자아와 타자의 관계, 섹슈얼리티, 의사소통의 난제, 개인 정체성에 관한 주제를 다뤄왔다. 아틸라의 대표작 중 하나인 〈수평-바카수오라〉(2011)의 '바카수오라'는 핀란드어로 '수평'을 의미한다. 6개의 영상 채널을 수평으로 이어서 구성한 이 영상설치 작품은 가문비나무의 모습을 최대한 변형하지 않고 영상촬영이라는 매커니즘을 통해 기록하려는 작가의 의도에서 제작되었다. 6개의 영상 채널은 마치 전통적인 초상화의 캔버스를 연상시킨다. 각각의 채널이 보여주는 바람에 미세하게 움직이는 나무는 그 푸르름과 가문비나무가 놓인 시간과 장소가 지닌 빛과 바람을 머금고 있으며, 커다란 나무의 전체를 이루는 부분이자 동시에 개별적인 것으로 존재한다. 우리는 영상을 바라보면서 거칠지 않은 바람 속에 흔들리는 거대한 나무 아래 서 있는 조그만 사람을 발견하게 된다. 아틸라는 이 작품에 관한 인터뷰를 통해 "비록 그 두 개(자연과 인간)가 이 세계에 공존하더라도 거기에는 이들이 평행적으로 존재하듯이 합일 될 수 없는 차이(discrepancy)가 있음을 보여준다."⁴고 언급했다. 이는 인간과 자연이라는 두 세계의 공존을 말하며 '우리가 서 있는 장소와 그 외 세계가 관계할 수 있는 가능한 부분을 찾는다'는 그의 작업 태도를 보여준다. 〈수평-바카수오라〉는 영상으로 대상을 기록하는 행위를 통해 실제 피사체와 영상 속 피사체의 관계, 나아가 영상 매커니즘과 기록하는 행위의 목적 간의 관계에 대해 고찰한다. 또한 자연의 기록이라는 것 역시 인간 중심적인 관점과 가치관 안에서 이루어진다는 것을 상기시키며, 동시에 나무의 초상이자 자연의 일부분인 한 생물을 기록하는 것에 대한 실험과 한계를 내포한다.

토마스 스트루스는 독일의 쿤스트아카데미 뒤셀도르프에서 회화와 사진을 전공하였고, 사진의 고전적 소재인 도시 전경, 자연 경관, 초상, 실내 풍경, 군중 등을 주변적 시선으로 응시하며 작가 특유의 적막한 사진 이미지 이면에 내포된 심리학적, 사회적 요소에 대해 말한다. 〈파라다이스 21, 주케이, 브라질 2001〉(2001)은 그가 2001년 브라질의 숲속에 들어가 그곳의 풍경, 특히 나뭇잎에 떨어져 아롱거리는 빛의 미묘한 변화를 포착한 작품이다. 거대한 우림의 부분을 포착한 이 작품은 깊고, 광활한 밀림의 전체와 내부를 상상하도록 한다.

테레시타 페르난데즈는 그가 경험한 다양한 문화와 역사적 특정성 그리고 서구의 식민주의와 포스트콜로니얼 시대의 권력 충돌 등과 같은 다양한 주제가 함축된 개념적 풍경작업으로 널리 알려진 작가이다. 특히 작가는 유성우, 북극광, 구름층, 불, 야광 등과 같은 자연현상을 적극적으로 작업의 소재로 삼으며 식민주의, 역사, 대지, 권력 등을 상징하는 금, 목탄, 광물을 주재료로 한 작업들을

제작해 왔다. 이번 전시에서 선보이는 〈어두운 땅(우주)〉(2019)은 작가가 지속적으로 탐구해 온 풍경과 장소의 재현이라는 주제를 더욱 폭넓게 확장시킨 작품이다. 페르난데즈의 풍경에 대한 깊은 고찰은 인간을 자연의 일부로 간주하고 인간과 자연의 조화를 추구한 전통적인 동양적 자연관에 근간을 두고 있으며, 이를 특정 문화·역사적 요소와 새로운 방식으로 접목한다. 예컨대 작가는 실제 특정 장소에서 채집된 광물을 재료로 사용하면서 그곳에 거주했던 사람들의 흔적이나 역사적 사건, 물리적으로 자연과 환경에 가해진 사실에 대한 기록을 함께 수집한다. 이 과정에서 발견된 광물이 있던 장소가 함의하는 본질적인 요소들을 다양하게 조합하여 전체론적인 관점이 투영된 풍경으로 재탄생 시킨다. 〈어두운 땅(우주)〉는 세 개의 금빛의 반사되는 크롬 판넬 위에 목탄을 촘촘하게 쌓아 올리고, 미세한 점들의 섬세한 묘사를 통해 자연의 거대 풍광을 연상시키는 이미지를 보여준다. 목탄 조각 하나하나는 전체의 풍경 안에서 개별적인 주체로 존재하기도 하면서 풍경이 지닌 오랜 역사를 우리 앞에 불러내기도 한다. 더하여 캔버스 역할을 하는 크롬판넬은 작품을 마주한 관람객들의 모습을 화면 안의 이미지들과 오버랩 하도록 비춘다. 이것은 관람객에게 작품과 작품을 둘러싼 공간에 대해 사적이고 개별적인 경험을 불러 일으키도록 하며 페르난데즈가 만들어낸 풍경 내부로 들어와 그곳에 존재하게 한다.

한국계 미국 작가 바이런 킴은 인종, 문화, 정체성에 대한 문제를 사적인 경험을 바탕으로 직관적이며 감성적인 조형언어로 담아내는 연작들을 선보여 왔다. 인간의 몸, 문화 혹은 자연 세계를 기본적인 작품의 소재로 삼으며 작가는 섬세하고 시적이며 통찰력 있는 작품들을 만들어왔다. 작가의 대표작인 〈제유법〉(1993), 〈명〉(2016) 등을 포함한 그의 회화 작업들은 때때로 미니멀리즘 혹은 추상표현주의 미학을 연상시키지만, 사적인 서사와 구체성을 띤 소재에서 출발한다는 면에서 사실주의에 근접해 보인다. 이번 전시에서는 바이런 킴이 2001년부터 작업을 시작하여 1,000점 넘게 그려 온 〈일요일 회화〉(2007-2016) 시리즈 34점을 선보인다. 작가는 매주 일요일마다 해가 지기 전의 하늘을 관조하며 그 풍경을 작가가 정한 특정한 크기(35.5×35.5cm)의 캔버스에 그린 후 작업이 완성된 일자와 장소 그리고 소회를 손 글씨로 기록하였다. 누구에게나 친숙한 자연의 이미지와 조합되는 사소하고 개인적인 일들의 기록들이 시간의 결 속에 집적되면서 제유의 방식을 통해 삶 전반에 대한 사유를 하게 만든다.

김세진은 현대사회를 살아가는 집단 혹은 군중 속의 개인이 거대한 사회 시스템과 패러다임 안에서 존재하는 방식과 삶의 태도에 주목해왔다. 이런 익명의 개인들이 갖는 고독과 불안, 단절은 영화적 언어와 다큐멘터리 의 방식을 차용한 작가의 영상 작업 속에 완성도 높은 시각언어로 그려진다. 〈2048〉(2020)은 2019년도 작가의 개인전에서 선보였던 신작을 이번 전시를 위해 새롭게 편집한 영상 작품이다. 이 작품은 김세진이 남극에 머물면서 직접 촬영한 남극에 대한 기록과 실제로 존재하지만 존재하지 않는 가상의 영토 "G"⁵에 관한 픽션이다. 작품의 제목인 '2048'은 해양을 평화와 연구의 목적으로만 이용하고, 영유권 선언 금지와 인류 공동 유산에 대한 보호에 관한

조약과 규정이 명시되어 있는 남극 조약이 만료되는 시점을 말한다. 남극은 지구에서 인류의 마지막 남은 미개척 대륙이자 지구에서 가장 추운, 그리고 다섯 번째로 큰 미지의 대륙이다. 엄청난 양의 자원이 매장되어 있는 것으로 추정되는 남극은 역사상 최초로 남극점에 도달했던 노르웨이 탐험가 로알 아문센(Roald Amundsen) 이후 세계 강대국들의 소유와 지배에 대한 욕망으로 점철되는 영토가 되었다. 김세진은 현재까지는 어떠한 국가도 차지하지 못하는 중립지역으로 선포된 남극이지만 가까운 미래에 도래할 인류의 예견된 분쟁과 갈등의 상황을 목도하며 "이상과 현실의 첨예한 대립이 양가적으로 존재하는 땅인 남극은 우리의 실재하는 현재와 미래의 유토피아이자 동시에 디스토피아를 역설적으로 보여준다."[6]고 말한다.

데이비드 내시는 1960년대 말 그가 유년시절에 많은 시간을 보냈던 북 웨일즈 블라이나이 페스니니오그(Blaenau Ffestingiog)에 정착하여 목재와 나무 그리고 자연환경을 작업의 근간으로 삼고 있다. 현재까지도 기원과 생성, 존재와 지속과 같은 자연의 섭리와 자연과 인간과의 관계에 관심을 두고 지속적인 작업을 해오고 있는 영국의 대표적인 조각가이다. 그는 특히 재해나 질병 등으로 불가피하게 손상된 나무만을 작품의 재료 사용하는데 이는 작가가 자연을 바라보는 관점과 생태예술가로서의 작업 태도를 보여준다. 후기 산업사회의 증상이 뚜렷하게 나타나기 시작한 1960년대 말, 자연의 훼손과 심각한 환경문제가 대두되면서 자연은 예술가들에게 항상 중요한 영감의 근원이었다. 데이비드 내시는 그 점을 인지하고, 기술의 발달과 소비문화의 가속화에 반하여 자연과 주변 환경에서 새로운 가능성을 모색했던[7] 생태미술가 그룹의 주요 일원으로 활동하였다. 작가는 "살아 있는 나무에 관심을 가지게 되고 직접 이를 심기 시작하자 나는 나무가 4가지 구성요소로 이루어진 산물이라는 것을 깨닫게 되었다. 나무는 광물이 풍부한 땅에 심어진다. 땅은 물질과 고형물질로 구성된 세상이다. 이들에게는 빛과 온기(불의 요소)가 필요하다. 나는 나무가 이 네 가지 요소(흙, 불, 물, 공기)가 잘 균형된 혼합물이라는 것을 깨달았다."[8]고 말한다. 그의 작업에 있어 나무는 시간, 삶의 순환과정, 그리고 소멸을 상징한다. 〈줄무늬의 달리는 사람〉(1989)은 가지가 사방으로 뻗어 나가는 나무둥치의 일부를 큰 변형 없이 그대로 이용하여 제작한 조각이다. 장인이 끌을 이용하여 작업하듯이 작가가 능숙하게 다루는 전기톱을 이용하여 원래 나무가 가지고 있는 줄기의 조형적 특징을 극대화 시키는 세밀한 표현과 더불어 재료에 대한 최소한의 개입을 통해 나무에 내재된 형상을 끌어내는 이 작품은 내시의 작업이 갖는 전형적인 특징을 보여준다.

현상의 부피

〈현상의 부피〉 섹션은 자연 현상에 대한 탐구와 이를 시각화한 작품들로 구성된다. 계절, 날씨, 물, 연기, 얼음, 공기 등의 자연적인 요소들은 미술의 소재이자 재료로서 오랫동안 탐색되고 실험되어 왔다. 부피가 없는 비물질적이고 일시적인 요소들은 예술가들에 의해 다양한 방식으로 가시화되고 조형성을

갖게 된다. 또한 시각적 차원을 넘어 경험적 차원의 관람을 제안하는 작품들은 자연에 대한 새로운 인지를 환기시킨다.

팀 프렌티스는 알루미늄이나 스테인리스 스틸과 같은 경량의 금속을 사용하여 공기의 흐름과 세기에 따라 즉각 반응하며 움직이는 조형 작업에 오랫동안 천착해왔다. 그는 이번 전시를 위해 국립현대미술관 서울 전시장 공용공간에 설치된 〈부드러운 비〉(2002)는 153개의 알루미늄 막대를 연결하여 여러 개의 모빌 형식으로 만들어 설치된 작품이다. 작가의 기존 작품과 유사한 작은 사각형의 알루미늄 조각들이 반복적으로 연결되어 기하학적인 구성을 보여주는 이 작품은 전시장 외부 복도공간의 천장에 설치되어 바람에 흔들리며 주변 환경에 즉각적으로 반응한다. 이것은 "공기의 움직임은 눈에 보이지 않지만 가장 아름다우며, 이런 공기의 움직임을 볼 수 있게 만드는 것이 자신의 작업"이라고 여기는 작가의 의도를 직관적으로 보여준다.

헤수스 라파엘 소토는 기술과 재료를 상대적으로 단순한 방식으로 작품에 적용하는 옵아트(optical art)와 키네틱 아트의 대가이다. 작가는 1950년대 초반부터 합성수지와 채색된 판들을 조합하여 시지각적 움직임을 구현하는 시네티즘(cinétisme) 조각을 연구하고 발전시켰다. 그 후 그는 1957년부터 투명체, 매달려 있는 물체, 움직이는 벽과 조각 등 '비물질화' 작업에 대한 형식적 실험을 지속했다. 수백 개의 면·선형의 합성수지를 매달아 연출한 공감각이 유실된 듯한 공간을 관람객이 '통과'하면서 균형 감각이 상실되는 순간에 역설적으로 되살아나는 그들의 퇴색되어버린 감각에 주목한다. 이번 전시에서는 국립현대미술관이 작품을 수집하고 과천관에서 장소특정적 작업으로 설치했던 이래로 약 20여년 만에 다시 소토의 〈파고들다〉(1988)를 선보인다. 소토가 "생선이 물속에 있듯이 우리는 세계 속에 있다."고 언급한 것과 같이 이 작품의 관람을 위해서 관람객은 단순한 시각적 관람자가 아닌 참여자로서 작품 속으로 들어가 천장에 매달린 2,000여 개의 비닐호스를 통과하는 과정을 경험하게 된다. 작품의 양 측면에서 비추는 조명등의 빛과 함께 파동 하듯이 보이는 비닐 호스들의 움직이는 효과는 관람자가 옵 아트의 경험적 차원을 느낄 수 있게 한다. 이는 시지각 현상을 보다 직접적으로 자극하는 방법이자 적극적인 관람 방식을 제안함으로써 관객의 새로운 감각을 일깨운다.

박기원은 공간성 자체를 작품의 소재이자 주제로 활용하는 한국의 대표적인 설치 미술가이다. 이번 전시에서 선보이는 〈넓이〉(2007-2008) 시리즈는 기하학적 색면으로 장지 위에 그린 회화 작업이다. 작가는 2000년대 초반부터 사계절을 주제로 100여 점 넘는 연작을 제작해 왔다. 이 연작의 일부인 〈넓이〉는 그림 화면을 크게 몇 개의 면으로 나누고, 각각의 면들을 서로 다른 방향의 결로 표현하여 다양한 시각에서 관찰한 공간 속 특정 장소의 상황을 표현했다. 색의 흐름은 감상자가 자연 속에서 사계를 연상하면서 크게 초록, 파랑, 갈색 계열로 연결하도록 구성된다. 화가들이 사계절을 그림의 소재로 삼았던 것은

17세기 프랑스 화가 니콜라 푸생(Nicolas Poussin)으로 오랜 역사를 거슬러 올라간다. 푸생은 사계절을 자연과 절기의 변화로 표현하는 것에[9] 그치지 않고 자연과 생명의 순환과 삶의 여정을 보여주었는데 박기원이 담은 계절의 색감 또한 비슷한 맥락으로 해석된다. 이 같은 박기원의 회화 작업은 감상자의 관점에서 처음에는 우선 하나의 커다란 색면으로 다가오지만 그림의 화면을 자세히 들여다보면 작가의 노동집약적인 '그리기'의 과정을 거쳐 그려진 면과 무수한 선의 중첩임을 알 수 있다. 박기원은 "장소와 작품 그리고 사람 간의 균형을 통해 현실과 비현실의 경계선으로 그들을 자연스럽게 이끌고자 한다."고 말한다. 그의 작업 전반이 장소의 원형성에 대한 탐구와 시간과 공간, 그리고 비물질적인 것들과 여백 사이의 경험에 관한 것이라고 할 수 있다. 같은 맥락에서 〈넓이〉는 평면작업 위에 시간과 공간성을 부여하는 회화인 동시에 20개의 연작이 연결되면서 완성되는 하나의 공간작업으로 확장된다고도 볼 수 있다. 구체적인 이미지 재현을 지양하는 박기원은 명상적이며 수행적인 반복을 통해 다양한 시각으로 관찰한 공간과 시간의 존재를 그림 화면에 담았다.

앤디 골즈워시는 대지미술(land art), 장소특정적(site-specific) 조각과 사진으로 주목받고 있는 영국의 생태예술가이자 환경운동가이다. 그는 1960년대 후반 현대미술이 지닌 틀과 경향 그리고 예술의 상업화에 따른 한계를 벗어나기 위해 전형적인 갤러리 공간을 거부하고, 광활한 대지 혹은 숲과 같은 자연에서 직접 작업을 제작했던 대표적인 생태환경미술가 중 한 명이다. 골즈워시는 60년대 당시부터 고드름, 나뭇잎, 꽃, 진흙, 잔가지, 가시덤불 등을 재배열한 작품들을 선보이며 널리 알려졌다. 작가는 여러 장소를 지나다니며 그날그날 제공되는 재료를 사용하는데 이는 어떤 장소에서 발견되길 원하는 무언가가 있다고 믿기 때문이라고 말한다. 또한 그는 자연에서 얻어진 특정 사물 그 자체만을 다루는 것이 아니라 그 사물이 가진 생명의 생성과 소멸, 그리고 그것을 둘러싼 환경과의 연관성까지 아우른다. 자연에서 채집된 재료들의 인위적인 배열, 혹은 조형적 구축과 설치로 구현되는 작가의 작업은 자연적 주변환경 속에 존재하면서 대비와 조화를 동시에 이루는 특징을 보여준다. 한편, 골즈워시의 작업들은 주변 자연물을 이용하는 속성으로 인해 소멸되기 쉽다는 점에서 '사진'이라는 매체가 매우 중요한 역할을 한다. 작품을 만드는 과정과 만들어진 상태, 시간이 지난 상태를 모두 사진으로 기록하는 것이다. 영구적인 작품을 제작할 때 작가는 인공적인 재료와 특수한 도구들을 사용하기도 하는데, 이번 전시에 선보이는 〈무제(흑)〉(1989)과 〈무제(백)〉(1989)가 그러한 작품이다. 유기적인 형태의 조각들을 둥글게 배열한 형상을 연상시키는 이 작품은 일시적이며, 단편적인 자연의 모습이 화면 안에서 영속화된 것 같은 느낌을 준다.

올라퍼 엘리아슨은 순수미술뿐만 아니라 시각예술 전반에서 다양하고 과감한 실험을 통해 자연, 과학, 철학 등 포괄적인 영역을 넘나드는 대표적인 현대미술가이다. 특히 그는 빛, 공기, 물, 온도 등의 자연요소를 이용한 유사-과학적(pseudo-scientific) 작품을 선보이며 물리적인 환경에 반응하는 인간의 감각작용에 대해 실험한다. 자연에서 오는 비가시적인 요소들 또는 움직임이나 빛, 반사, 색채의 조합 등을 이용한 설치작업들은 물리적인 공간과 상호 작용을 일으키는가 하면, 때때로 작품이 놓이는 장소를 전혀 다른 공간으로 변모시키면서 관람객들에게 새로운 차원의 인식과 경험을 제공한다. 122개의 복잡한 다면체의 구조로 이루어진 구(sphere) 형상의 조각작품인 〈사각 구체〉(2007)는 작가가 자주 사용하는 반사되는 재료를 이용하여 제작되었다. 이 작품은 관람객 눈높이에 맞도록 공중에 설치되어 작품의 내부로 무한하게 확장되는 시각적 경험을 불러일으킨다. 또한 거울 같은 표면에 비친 빛이 바닥과 벽면에 다양한 형태로 반사되면서 작품 자체가 공간으로까지 확장된다. 기하학적인 형태에 대한 탐구는 엘리아슨의 작업에서 중요한 부분으로 작용한다. 작가는 작업활동 초기에 건축가와 수학자와의 협업을 통해 이를 발전시켰으며, 현재는 그의 스튜디오에 기하학적 구조를 연구하는 더욱 전문화된 팀을 두고 작업하고 있다. 이 작품은 그의 기하학적, 경험적 조형실험을 보여주는 전형적인 작품 중 하나이다.

한스 하케는 미국을 기반으로 활동하는 독일 출신의 개념미술가로서 제도비판미술의 한 전형을 제시한 작가로 잘 알려져 있다. 하케는 "어떤 것이 자연스럽다(natural)는 것은 두 가지를 의미하는데, 이것은 '자연'과 연관된다. 이 의미는 스스로 이해되는(self-understood), 보통의(ordinary), 구속받지 않은 (uncontrived), 평균의(normal), 어떤 일상의 질(quality)을 가진 것"[10]이라고 언급한 바 있다. 이 같은 그의 생각은 형식적, 개념적 측면에서 작가의 작업 전반에 나타난다. 그는 응축, 강수, 증발, 온도 변화에 따른 팽창과 수축처럼 자연 에너지를 다양한 실험을 통해 하나의 작품으로 구현하고자 했는데, 이는 1950년대 그가 참여했던 예술그룹 제로(ZERO)의 움직이는 물질에 대한 관심과 맥을 함께한다. 하케는 자신의 아이디어를 실현하기 위해서 기술의 필요성을 느꼈고, E.A.T.[11]를 통해 공학자를 소개받아 협업했다. 그 결과 빛, 온도, 습도 등 주변 환경에 반응하는 장치인 〈아이스 테이블〉(1967)을 제작했다. 이 작품은 1967년 E.A.T.가 주최한《더 많은 시작: 예술과 기술의 실험》에서 처음 선보였으며, 2018년 국립현대미술관에서 열린《예술과 기술의 실험(E.A.T.): 또 다른 시작》전에 출품된 바 있다.

장소의 이면

서양 미술사에서 말하는 '풍경'은 인간의 인위적인 영향력이 가해진 자연의 모습을 포괄적으로 말한다. 프랑수와 줄리앙은 풍경에 관한 그의 저서에서 "풍경을 이루는 것이 세상 전체를 담아내고 있다면, 그 장소는 그 자체로 전체가 되어 상호 작용과 소통을 끝없이 일으킨다 하겠다."[12]고 말했다. 〈장소의 이면〉 섹션은 '장소'는 '어떠한 일이 일어나는 곳 또는 어떤 일을 하는 곳'이라는 사전적 의미를 상기한다. 특히, 하나의 장소를 담은 풍경의 이면에서 벌어지는 현재진행형의 역설과 근접한 미래, 그리고 역사에 대한 고찰을 담은 작품들을 보여준다.

한성필은 사진과 비디오를 기반으로 다양한 문화에 대한 이해와 접근을 통해 환상과 허구, 실재와 재현, 거짓과 진실의 혼동에서 발현되는 인식론적 착란에 대해 이야기한다. 이번 전시에서는 작가의 〈그라운드 클라우드〉(2005/2012) 시리즈 3점을 선보인다. 한적해 보이는 전원 정경 속에 푸른 하늘을 가로지르는 흰 연기가 인상적인 이 작품은 실제 프랑스 노장-쉬르-센에 위치한 프랑스의 가장 큰 원전 중의 하나인 원자력 발전소가 있는 풍경이다. 평화로워 보이는 농촌 마을에 청명한 하늘과 들판을 관통하며 퍼지는 거대한 굴뚝에서 나오는 수증기는 평화와 공포, 그리고 물질문명의 이기의 대표적 산물인 원자력 발전소가 공존하는 기묘한 장면을 연출한다. 이러한 풍경은 '현실이지만 초현실적 미장센'으로 변환되며 원자력에 대한 이상적 이해와 현실에 직면하면서 표출되는 감성적 반응 사이의 차이와 경계를 보여준다.

로랑 그라소는 다층적 시간성, 초자연 현상, 집단 공포 등 인간 의식에 영향을 미치는 다양한 비가시적 힘을 드로잉, 페인팅, 설치, 조각, 비디오 등의 매체로 시각화함으로써 역사와 현실을 새롭게 바라보기를 시도한다. 그라소는 비가시적인 것들을 통해 가시적 세계를 조망함으로써 일종의 공통성을 도출해낸다. 이것은 과학적인 관점이나 과학을 초월하는 우주적 관점, 혹은 과거에서 미래, 또는 미래에서 과거로의 이동을 허용하는 듯한 다차원적인 관점에서 묘사된다. 〈무성영화〉(2010)는 로랑 그라소가 8회 마니페스타에서 선보였던 작품이다. 이 영상은 스페인 코르도헤나의 해안 군사지대를 촬영한 것으로 바다와 그 주위를 둘러싼 평온해 보이는 해안 풍경이 점진적으로 그 주변을 둘러싼 위장(camouflaged)된 군사시설물을 드러내는 화면들로 이어진다. 화면에서는 비록 평화롭고 경치 좋은 해안을 보여주는 듯하지만 페르소나가 부재하는 풍경 속의 군사시설들을 통해 과거 역사의 지나온 흔적과 현재를 말한다. 그리고 바다의 수면 위로 간간이 모습을 드러내는 검은 잠수정은 미래에 일어날 수 있는 잠재적 충돌을 암시한다. 군사해안선에 드리운 긴장감이 응축되어 있는 장면을 담은 이 영상은 보이는 것과 보이지 않는 것, 가까이 혹은 멀리에서 공격하는 측과 포위하는 측, 그리고 외부의 시선과 내부의 시점을 오가는 양가적인 관점을 보여준다. 이 작품은 보이지 않는 현실의 이면에 존재하는 진실과 역설을 작가의 언어로 시각화하기 위해 탐색하고 실험하는 그라소의 대표작 중의 하나이다.

맵 오피스는 각각 작가와 건축가인 로랑 구티에레즈와 발레리 폭트패가 결성한 홍콩을 기반으로 활동하는 작가 그룹이다. 이들은 사진, 회화, 설치, 공연, 문학 및 이론적 텍스트 등의 매체를 통해 물리적, 상상적 영역을 유연한 시각으로 연구하는 작업을 보여주면서 아시아 지역을 바라보는 다양한 비판적 시각의 가능성을 탐색해왔다. 이번 전시에서는 국립현대미술관이 소장한 이후 처음으로 선보이는 〈유령 섬〉(2019) 영상과 사진, 그리고 엽서와 지도를 선보인다. 〈유령 섬〉은 유사 이래 인간이 생존을 위해 바다에서 행해 왔던 수많은 어업과 관련된 활동에 관심을 두고 그와 관련된 사회적, 경제적, 역사적 관점의 이야기와 다양한 문화들에 대해 조사하는 진행형의 프로젝트이다.

이 작품은 아시아의 각기 다른 지역에 설치된 예술 네트워크의 일부로서 진행되었으며, 바다에 버려지거나 유실된 어망 같은 해양 쓰레기와 바다, 산호 생물 등의 해양 생태계에 대한 문제를 다룬다. 〈유령섬〉는 2017년 제1회 방콕비엔날레 전시를 위해 제작되었으며 태국의 크래비(Krabi) 지방 해안의 만조와 간조가 일어나는 바다에 4개월 간 설치되었던 6미터 높이의 거대한 조형물과 영상 작업이다. 오랜 역사 속에서 인간이 생존을 위해 어업활동을 지속하는 동안 그물의 사용은 기원전으로 그 역사를 거슬러 올라간다. 현대에 들어와서 합성물질로 제작되는 그물은 오늘날에도 지속적으로, 그리고 과도하게 사용되고 있다. 어업활동을 위한 그물의 본래의 목적은 물고기를 잡아올리는 것이나 현재 바다에 버려지고 유실된 그물(ghost net)은 그와 정반대로 바닷속의 물고기를 비롯한 다양한 생물들을 가두어 두면서 바다 생태계를 위협하고 있다. 이 공공 프로젝트의 설치물을 제작하면서 약 300킬로그램 무게의 유실된 그물들을 수거하여 업사이클링하였는데, 주변 해안의 쓰레기를 수거하고 재활용하면서 일종의 해양 에코시스템을 회복하는 정화 작업이 일어났다. 〈유령섬〉 영상 작품에 기록된 조형물은 주변 해안의 섬들과 흡사한 형태를 띠며, 작가들에 의해 제작된 이 인공의 섬은 실재하는 섬들 속에서 그 지역 해안 지형을 바꾸었다. 이 작품은 아시아 지역의 커뮤니티에 대한 새로운 접근과 인간의 활동으로 무너지는 해양생태의 회복에 대한 목소리를 내고자 하는 의미를 담고 있다.

원성원은 각기 다른 시공간에서 찍은 사진 이미지를 섬세하게 중첩시키는 콜라주 작업을 통해 현실과 공상이 뒤섞인 독특한 내러티브를 만들어내는 작품으로 알려져 있다. 작가는 그가 표현하고자 하는 '타인'의 영역을 깊숙이 탐사하기 위해 현대를 살아가는 7개의 전문직업군(언론인, IT전문가, 교수, 약사, 금융인, 공직자, 연구원)을 정하고, 이들에 관한 다양한 관점과 시각을 실재하는 풍경에서 채집한 이미지 조각을 섬세하게 조합한 풍경에 함축하는 작업을 해왔다. 그는 각각의 직업을 탐구하면서 각 직업을 바라보는 표피적인 시선 속에 숨겨진 다양한 모습을 발견하게 된다. 작가는 각각의 직업군을 상징하는 이미지들을 수집하기 위해 2년간 전국을 돌며 수 천 장의 사진을 촬영하였다. 이렇게 수집된 수많은 고해상도 사진들은 작가의 세심한 포토샵 작업을 통해 지상에는 존재하지 않는 가상의 풍경으로 재탄생 된다. 이 같은 원성원의 아날로그적인 촬영 방식과 노동집약적인 사진 콜라주 작업은 스케일과 디테일을 동시에 지닌, 관객을 압도하는 힘과 완성도를 보여준다. 〈언론인의 바다〉(2017)에 등장하는 바다는 거대한 파도와 태풍이 몰아치는 풍광이다. 흡사 거대한 자연이 보여주는 공포와 아름다움을 동시에 갖는 숭고미 속에 인간의 무력함을 보여주는 터너(J. M. W. Turner)의 회화를 연상시킨다. 파도가 거세게 몰아치는 바다 위에서 위태롭게 배를 타고 있는 하이에나(언론인)가 바라보는 파도와 고정된 섬에서 고정된 시선을 가진 펭귄(역시 언론인)이 바라보는 파도 사이에는 어떤 간극이 존재하는 듯하다. 원성원은 이런 생생한 바다의 이미지를 채집하기 위해 세 차례의 태풍을 겪으며

위험을 무릅쓰고 폭풍의 경로를 쫓았다. 그렇게 집적되고 재조합 된 수많은 파도들은 다양한 시간과 공간을 동시에 담고 있다. 〈IT 전문가의 물-풀 네트워크〉(2017)는 가상의 영역에서 존재하는 데이터와 수많은 네트워크 속에서 새로운 가치를 찾고, 만들어내는 IT 전문가들의 모습을 풍경으로 담은 작품이다. 작가는 온라인상에서 벌어지는 비가시적인 데이터의 흐름을 강가의 빽빽이 자란 물풀로 표현하였다. 물풀의 물결에 따라 움직이는 모습은 수심에 존재하는 보이지 않는 물의 정보를 포함하고 가시화한다. 물의 양이 늘어나면 물풀들은 물의 속도와 방향에 맞춰 거대한 물풀의 흐름을 형성하는데 이러한 모습은 온라인상에서 벌어지는 문화와 유행의 흐름과 유사하다. 다양한 종(種)의 조류(鳥類)들은 물풀의 거대한 흐름을 주의깊게 탐색하며, 파악하는 IT 전문가들의 모습을 담고 있다.

1   프랑수와 줄리앙, 『풍경에 대하여』, 김설아 옮김, 아모르문디, 서울, 2016, 13쪽.
2   마순자, 『자연, 풍경, 그리고 인간』, 아카넷, 파주, 2003, 56쪽.
3   프랑수와 줄리앙, 앞의 책, 17쪽.
4   앨리슨 버틀러 외, 『Eija-Liisa Ahtila, Parallel Worlds』, 슈타이들, 괴팅겐, 2012, 23쪽
5   가상의 영토 G는 현재 남반구의 땅 전체를 포함하던 과거의 초대륙인 곤드와나(Gondwana)를 의미한다.
6   김세진 작가노트
7   마순자, 앞의 책, 279쪽. 저자는 "후기 산업 사회의 증상이 나타나기 시작하는 이 시기에 자연환경이 예술가들에게 차츰 중요하고 새로운 관심의 대상으로 부상한 것은 자연스러운 결과였다. 풍경이 인간과 함께 서양의 예술가들에게 항상 영감의 중요한 근원이었던 점을 생각할 때 테크놀로지와 소비문화, 미술을 위한 미술 등의 언어에 대한 식상한 일군의 작가들이 자연과 주변 환경에서 새로운 가능성을 모색했던 것은 시대의 징후를 앞서 읽는 예술가들의 전위적 전통이었다고 할 수 있을 것이다."라고 언급하였는데 데이비드 내시는 이 같은 생태미술가 그룹의 주요 작가로 활동하였다.
8   앤드류 람비스·데이비드 내시, 『David Nash』 국제갤러리, 서울, 2007, 31쪽.
9   마순자, 앞의 책, 82쪽. "푸생의 〈사계절〉은 절기를 그리는 달력 그림의 전통에서 비롯된 것이다. 그러나 푸생은 계절에 따른 자연의 변화와 풍속의 의미의 전달에 국한하고 있지 않다. 그의 사계는 하루의 네 시기, 그리고 인생의 여정을 상징한다. 해 뜨는 신선한 아침, 한낮의 밝은 태양, 풍요로운 오후의 시간, 그리고 어두워지는 해질녘의 묘사는 네 계절뿐만 아니라 하루의 네 시기의 묘사이며, 동시에 탄생에서 죽음에 이르는 인생 여정의 상징이다. 푸생은 이 그림들에서 자연의 변화에 따른 색조의 다양한 범주와 미묘한 빛의 상태를 정확히 그리고자 노력하였다."
10 제프리 카스트너(편), 『Nature』, 화이트채플 갤러리; MIT프레스, 런던; 캠브리지, 매사추세츠, 2012, 28쪽.
11 E.A.T.(Experiments in Art and Technology)는 1966년 미국 뉴욕에 설립된 미술과 과학의 융합을 선구적으로 이끌어낸 비영리 단체이다.
12 프랑수와 줄리앙, 앞의 책, 244쪽.

AXIS OF HORIZON

Okkum Yang, Curator,
National Museum of Modern and Contemporary Art, Korea

Axis of Horizon is a special exhibition centering on international art from the collection of the National Museum of Modern and Contemporary Art, Korea (MMCA). This exhibition was designed to focus on "nature" – a traditional subject matter and theme that has long been explored and used for artistic representation between the Renaissance and the modern era – as it reinterprets it from a contemporary perspective and examines it in different ways.

Obscured within the context of Western art history by themes derived from religion and human-centric thinking, nature was not actively addressed by artists until the 17th century, when landscape art became established as an independent subject. As François Jullien writes, "Landscape painting was, as we know, born of a change in the art, but for a long time before then all it did was fill the 'empty corners.' It was background, decor. It made but slow progress in European art, wriggle free of the hegemony of 'history': that is, of both the significance of 'action' (Félibien) and the ideal beauty incarnate in the body (Lessing)."[1] The *Axis of Horizon* exhibition shares approaches to nature that underwent a continuous transformation in the wake of landscape painting, which treated nature as an object of subjective art for the first time. This encompasses not only explorations of nature based on reinterpretations that took shape amid the aesthetic experiments of contemporary art, but also the relationship between nature and human beings, society, the individual, and history.

While the Eastern perspective has traditionally pursued nature in a state that has not been subjected to artificial forces, the Western one has treated nature as something to be conquered.[2] The "landscape" as we ordinarily refer to it connotes nature that has been developed or transformed into different forms of civilized states. The concept of the "Arcadia" as a primeval, ideal form of nature has existed throughout the long history of Europe – but even this idea of beautiful, abundant utopia springs from a view of nature that centers on human ideals. This exhibition seeks to use aesthetic explorations and representation of nature to examine the different layers that exist underneath what is visible. It shares a wide and multifarious range of approaches that range from juxtaposing the past and present implied by landscapes as they can be interpreted within a cultural and historical context to evoking the coexistence of nature and humanity, with the phenomena of nature and its invisible elements visualized or reinterpreted as artwork in and of themselves.

The title *Axis of Horizon* refers to a framework in which the horizontal point at which the sky meets the earth or sea is posited as "nature," as we attempt to establish an axis to portray our different coordinates of perception with regard to it. The positing of the "horizon" as a symbol of nature may be connected to the concept of regarding the horizon as "delimiting" nature.[3] The "axis" here exists at a boundary that is like a window or thresholds for viewing nature at a different perception, affording a new perspective that flexibly crosses the borders between inside and outside of nature or between human beings and civilization.

This exhibition illustrates the aesthetic practice of nature and the rivalry that formed between human beings and nature over the course of history through works that range from traditional media such as painting and sculpture to more diverse media such as photography, multi-media, and installation. Additionally, it seeks to reflect on and envision the future through the implicit messages of contemporary art with the depiction and representation and nature, the contemplation of life, and the awareness that we humans too are part of nature.

The Whole of Parts

The word "part" necessarily entails subordination to the concept of a "whole." A part is a whole in itself, in that exists separately as one thing, and larger wholes are formed through the combination of different parts that function as parts of a whole. The exhibition's opening section, titled "The Whole of Parts," consists of works of art having to do with insights into life itself as achieved through fragmentary representations of nature. Works that illustrate human limitations and coexistence as parts of nature help awaken our perceptions of history, the present, and the future. They may also be seen as showing us how to approach fundamental question by means of the synecdoche of nature.

Jennifer Steinkamp has used computer animation and video media to produce works that experiment in new ways with architectural spaces, movement, and phenomenological perception. In particular, she has focused on changes in phenomenological perception, where the boundaries between actual space and illusion become blurred as 3D animation videos of abstract organic movements originating from natural elements are projected in specific settings. *Still-Life 3* (2019) is one of the recent works from the artist's *Still-Life* series, which she has been producing since 2016. The artist has attempted to break with the old practice of depicting flowers and fruit as still-life work — particularly among the Dutch and Flemish paintings of the 16th century, whose Vanitas paintings metaphorically represented values of stillness and the finiteness of life. To this end, she fills a virtual space with the fruit and flowers one might expect to find in a still-life, evoking the energy of life and natural vitality as they float about and collide.

Eija-Liisa Ahtila, one of Finland's renowned visual artists and filmmakers, presents a broad range of work that includes video installations incorporating moving images as well as films, photographs, and drawings. Early on, the artist focused on conceptual work originating in art theory, institutional critique, and feminism. Since the 1990s, however, she has turned her attention to images, language, narrative, and spatial construction, focusing on issues having to do with the relationship between the self and others, sexuality, communication difficulties, and individual identity. One of Ahtila's most representative works is *Horizontal-Vaakasuora* (2011), where the word "vaakasuora" is Finnish for "horizon." Consisting of six horizontally linked video channels, this video installation was created with the aim of using video as a mechanism to record a spruce tree with a minimum of alteration. The six video channels call to mind the canvas of a traditional portrait painting. Shown on the channels, the tree sways in the wind, with its subtle shades of green and the colors and air flows of the time and place where the spruce is situated, existing both individually and as part of the whole that is the larger tree. Watching the video, we see a tiny person standing at the base of this enormous tree as it sways in a gentle breeze. Speaking about this work in an interview, Ahtila said, "There is discrepancy so that, even if [nature and humanity] do exist in this world together, they are parallel."[4] This illustrates

her approach to artistic work: speaking of the coexistence of the two worlds represented by nature and humanity, she says that she "seeks the parts where the places we stand and the outside world can relate." Through the recording of an object in the video medium, *Horizontal-Vaakasuora* examines the relationship between the actual object and the object within the film — and between the film mechanism and the purpose of the act of recording. It also calls attention to the fact that the recording of nature takes places within a human-centered perspective and value system, while encompassing an experiment with the documentation of a tree and portrayal of an organism within nature, as well as its attendant limitations.

Thomas Struth studied painting and photography at the Kunstakamedie Düsseldorf in Germany. Examining classical subject matter of photography from a peripheral perspective — cityscapes, natural scenery, portraits, indoor landscapes, crowd scenes, and so forth — he addresses the psychological and social elements that lie beyond his characteristically desolate images. For *Paradise 21, Yuquehy, Brazil 2001* (2001), he ventured into the forest in Brazil to represent the landscape there, in particular the subtle changes in light mottling the leaves on the trees. Capturing one portion of a broad and vast forest, the work leads the viewer to imagine the whole of this deep and expansive jungle and what lies inside.

As an artist, Teresita Fernández is widely known for her conceptual landscape works, which incorporate different themes such as the different cultures and singularities of history that she has experienced and the clashing of powers within Western colonialism and the postcolonial era. In particular, she has drawn actively on natural phenomena as subject matter — including meteor showers, the northern lights, cloud layers, fire, and nightscapes — to produce work that chiefly incorporates metal, charcoal, and minerals as symbols of colonialism, history, the earth, and power. *Dark Earth (Cosmos)* (2019), which appears in this exhibition, represents a broader expansion of a theme consistently explored by the artist, namely the "representation of landscapes and places." Fernández's profound examination of landscapes is based in the traditional Eastern view of nature, which regards human beings as part of nature and seeks unity and harmony between them. In her artwork, this is then applied to specific cultural and historical elements and new approaches. For instance, the artist has made use of minerals actually extracted from a particular location, while collecting evidence of the people who inhabited it along with archival information about historical incidents and the phenomena physically visited upon nature and the environment. In different ways, she blends the essential elements inherent to the places where minerals existed in the past as discovered within this process, using them to newly create a landscape reflecting a holistic perspective. For her *Dark Earth (Cosmos),* she densely stacks charcoal on three chrome panels reflecting a gold sheen; with her finely detailed depiction of tiny dots, she presents an image that evokes a vast natural landscape. Each piece of charcoal exists as an individual subject within the overall landscape, while summoning that landscape's long history before us. Serving as "canvases," the chrome panels reflect the faces of the work's viewers so that they overlap with the images on them. This leads the viewers to draw upon their personal and individual experiences of the work and the space surrounding it — entering into the landscape that Fernández has created and existing inside of it.

The Korean-American artist Byron Kim has produced series of works that incorporate issues of ethnicity, culture, and identity into an intuitive and artistic language rooted in personal experience. Adopting human bodies, culture, and the natural world as his basic subject matter, the artist has created artwork that is subtle, poetic, and insightful. His most representative works include paintings such as *Synecdoche* (1993) and *Bruise* series (2016), which sometimes evoke the aesthetics of Minimalism or Abstract Expressionism — yet are also akin to Realism in that they originate in subject matter with a personal narrative and a concrete quality. This exhibition features 34 works from his *Sunday Paintings* series (2007–2016), an ongoing effort that began in 2001 and has seen Kim produce over 1,000 paintings. Each Sunday, the artist has observed the sky just before sundown, painting the landscape onto a canvas of prescribed dimensions (35.5×35.5 cm) and recording the date and place of its completion along with a brief handwritten journal entry or personal impression. The records of small, personal things combine with images of nature that are familiar to anyone, collecting within the texture of time to form a synecdoche that leads us to contemplate life in general.

Sejin Kim has focused on the ways in which the individual members of modern society's groups or crowds exist within vast social systems and paradigms, along with their attitudes about living. The solitude, anxiety, and disconnection of these anonymous individuals are represented in a highly developed visual language within the artist's single-channel HD video work, which incorporates cinematic language and documentary techniques. The video piece *2048* (2020), a new work shown by the artist at a 2019 solo exhibition that has been newly edited for this exhibition, combines records of Antarctica filmed by the artist during her stay there with fictional content about an imaginary territory known as "G" that exists but does not exist.[5] The year "2048" in the work's title refers to the expiration date of the Antarctic Treaty, which states that the seas are only to be used for peaceful and research-related purposes and includes regulations and facts barring the declaration of territorial rights and protecting shared human heritage. Antarctica is an unknown continent — the last continent on earth to remain undeveloped by humankind, the coldest on the planet and the fifth largest. Believed to contain vast quantities of buried resources, it is a territory that the world's powers have sought to own or dominate ever since the Norwegian explorer Roald Amundsen became the first person to reach the South Pole. While Antarctica has thus far been declared a neutral region not claimed by any country, Sejin Kim bears witness to the human conflict and strife that is predicted to arise over it in the near future. "As a place where a heated conflict between ideals and reality exists in an ambivalent sense, Antarctica shows the reality that exists for us now, the utopia of the future, and at the same time, ironically, a dystopia," the artist has explained.[6]

David Nash deals with wood, trees, and the natural environments as central elements in his work. In the late 1960s, he settled in Blaenau Ffestiniog, a town in northern Wales where he had spent a lot of time in his early childhood. Since then, he been one of Great Britain's preeminent sculptors, producing ongoing work with a focus on the relationship between nature and human beings and natural principles such as origins, genesis, existence, and continuation. For his work, he uses only wood that had been unavoidably damaged through disaster or disease — a fact that exemplifies his perspective on nature and his approach as an ecological artist. With the destruction of nature and severe environment issues emerging in the late 1960s as the symptoms of late industrial society became increasingly evident, nature has consistently served as an important source of inspiration to artists. In recognition of this, he became active as a key member of an ecological artists' group seeking out new possibilities within nature and the environment in the face of technological developments and the onrush of consumer culture.[7] The artist has explained, "Once I started looking more into the living tree and began to plant them, I saw how they are a weave of the four elements. The trees are seeded in the earth, which is full of minerals. That's a world of matter and solids. They need light and warmth (which is the fire element) and they need water and air. I realize that wood is a very balanced amalgam of these four elemental forces (Earth, Fire, Water and Air)."[8] In Nash's work, trees symbolize time, the cyclical process of life, and extinction. His *Striped Runner* (1989) is a sculpture in which a portion of tree trunk with branches extending is all directions has been incorporated without any major alternations. It illustrates the typical characteristics of Nash's work: like an artisan working with a chisel, the artist skillfully employs a chainsaw to produce intricate expression that maximally heights the artistic aspects of the tree's original trunk, while his minimal interference with the materials helps to bring out the inherent form of the wood.

- - - - - - - - - - -
The Volume of Phenomena

The section "The Volume of Phenomena" consists of explorations of natural phenomena and artworks that visualize them. Natural elements like the seasons, weather, water, smoke, ice, and air have long been explored and experimented with as subject matter and materials for art. Non-material, fleeting elements without volume have taken on artistic qualities as they have been visualized in different ways by artists, while artwork that suggests possibilities for experiential appreciation beyond the visual have helped to awaken new perceptions of nature.

Tim Prentice has used lightweight metals such as aluminum and stainless steel to produce sculpture that move in immediate response to the flow of air and its intensity. For this exhibition, his work *Soft Rain* (2002) has been placed in the public space at MMCA Seoul. This installation work consists of several mobile shape formed by linking 153 aluminum rods. Similar to the artist's past works, the small, rectangular aluminum fragments are repeatedly connected to produce a geometric composition that has been attached to the ceiling of the gallery's exterior corridor space, where it sways in the wind, reacting instantly to its surrounding environment. It is an intuitive illustration of the aim of the artist, who has said that the movement of the air, though not visible to the eyes, is the most beautiful thing — and that it is his seek to make that movement of the air visible.

Jesús Rafael Soto was a master of optical art and kinetic art, incorporating technology and materials into his work in relatively simple ways. In the early 1950s, he began studying and developing a cinétisme approach to sculpture, in which visual movement was achieved through the combination of synthetic resin and colored panels. In 1957, he began his ongoing formal experimentation with "dematerialization," including transparent forms, dangling objects, and moving walls and sculptures. As viewers pass through spaces that seem stripped of their synesthesia with hundreds of dangling lines and planes of synthetic resin, they come to focus on the decolorized sense, which ironically becomes reawakened at the moment the sense of equilibrium is lost. For this exhibition, *Penetrable* (1988) is being shown for the first time in around two decades since it was acquired by MMCA and installed as a site-specific work at MMCA Gwacheon. Soto said that "we exist in the world as fish do in water" — and to appreciate this work, the viewer cannot remain a simple visual observer, but must enter the work as a participant and experience the process of passing through the 2,000 plastic hoses dancing from the ceiling. The effect of the hoses' movement as they seem to ripple with the colors of the lights shone on either side of the work allows the viewer to sense the experiential dimension of optical art. This is both a way of more strongly stimulating visual phenomena and an attempt to awaken new senses in the viewer by suggesting a three-dimensional approach to art appreciation.

Kiwon Park is one of Korea's prominent installation artists, treating spatiality itself as a major theme and subject matter for his art. This exhibition includes work from his *Width* series (2007-2008) of paintings in geometric color planes on Korean *jangji* paper. Since the early over 2000s, the artist has produced a series of 100 paintings on the theme of "the four seasons." Created as part of this series, *Width* has the situation of a specific location observed within space from multiple angles. It is divided into four planes, with repeated small lines in different directions onto paper. The flow of color is arranged to proceed generally through green, blue, and brown colors, recalling the four seasons of nature for the viewer. The selection of the four seasons as a subject matter for paintings has a long history dating back to the 17th century French artist Nicolas Poussin. Rather than simply representing the seasons through changes in nature and solar terms, Poussin presented the cycles of nature and vitality and the journey of life. The color tones of the seasons that Kiwon Park presents can be interpreted along similar lines.[9] From the viewer's perspective, Park's painting appears at first like one large color field painting — but a closer look at the painting shows how the plane was produced through a labor-intensive working process by the artist, and how innumerable lines have been overlaid within it. "Through the balance among setting, artwork, and person, I am attempting to draw them naturally toward the boundary between reality and unreality," the artist has said. His work as a whole could be characterized as concerned with explorations of the original nature of places; with time and space; and with non-material things and experiences within the margins. In this context, *Width* is both a painting that imbues temporal and spatial aspects into a two-dimensional work, and at the same time expands into a spatial artwork that achieves completion as the series of 20 paintings is brought together. Abstaining from concrete representation of images, Kiwon Park has captured the existence of space and time as observed from different angles, bringing it onto the painting through meditative and performative repetition.

Andy Goldsworthy is a British environmental artist and activist who has drawn notice for his work in land art and site-specific sculpture and photography. He is considered one of the leading environmental artists who rejected the conventional gallery space to produce works of art in the vastness of land and natural environments such as forests as a way of breaking beyond the frameworks and tendencies of contemporary art in the late 1960s and transcending the limitations imposed by the commercialization of art. Goldsworthy is widely known for his artworks since the 1960s, which have involved the rearrangement of icicles, leaves, flowers, earth, branches, and brambles. The artist has explained that he uses the materials provided to him from day to day as he passed through different places, as he believes "there is something in a place that wants to be discovered." He does not only focus on the specific objects he obtains from nature, however, but also on the object's life — its emergence and extinction — and its relation to its surrounding environment. Consisting of artificial arrangements of materials gathered from nature or of sculptural constructions and installations, his work is also characterized by the way it achieves both harmony and contrast as it exists within its natural environment. Because he does use objects from the natural environment, many of his works are perishable — which means that the medium of photograph plays a very important role in them. Goldsworthy uses photographs to record the process of his artwork's creation and the resulting work in its finished state as well as its state after time has passed. The artist also makes use of artificial materials and special tools when he is producing work of a permanent character, a category into which this exhibition's *Untitled (Black)* (1989) and *Untitled (White)* (1989) fall. Calling to mind a round arrangement of sculptures with organic shapes, the works convey the sense of fleeting, fragmentary images from nature having been perpetualized within the canvas.

Olafur Eliasson is a leading contemporary artist who works in the full range of domains — including nature, science, and philosophy — as he pursues bold and eclectic experiments not only in the fine arts but in all of the visual arts. In particular, he has experiments with human sensory responses to physical environments through "pseudo-scientific" work incorporating natural elements such as light, air, water, and temperature. Utilizing invisible elements from nature as well as movement, light, reflection, and combinations of colors, his installation works generate interactions with physical space; other times, he provides viewers with new dimensions of perception and experience by transforming the environment where his work is situations into a completely different space. His *Square Sphere* (2007), a spherical sculpture consisting of a complex 122-faced polyhedral structure, was produced with reflective materials that the artist has often employed. Installed in midair so that it faces the viewer at eye level, the work shows space expanding infinitely inside of it. At the same time, the work itself expands into space as the lights reflected on its mirror-like surface are reflected in different ways off of the floor and walls. Explorations of geometric shapes make up an important part of Eliasson's work. In his early career, he developed them in collaboration with an architect and mathematician; these days, he has a specialized team at work researching geometric structures in his studio. This piece may be seen as a typical illustration of his geometric, experiential experiments with sculpture.

Hans Haacke is a German-born, US-based conceptual artist who is well known for providing a model of institutionally critical art. "[Natural] has an intended double meaning," the artist has said. "It refers to 'nature,' and it means something self-understood, ordinary, uncontrived, normal, something of an everyday quality."[10] His ideas are visible throughout his works in both formal and conceptual terms. With his different experiments, he has attempted to create artwork from the energy of nature, such as the expansions and contractions associated with condensation, precipitation, evaporation, and temperature change. This echoes the interest in "moving substances" of the artists' group ZERO, which he participated in during the 1950s. Sensing that he needed technology to realize his ideas, Haacke collaborated with an engineer whom he met through E.A.T.[11] The result of this was *Ice Table* (1967), a mechanism that responded to features of the surrounding environment such as light, temperature, and moisture. Presented for the first time in 1967 at the E.A.T.-organized exhibition *Some More Beginnings: Experiments in Art and Technology,* the work was shown again in 2018 at MMCA in the exhibition *E.A.T. (Experiments in Art and Technology): Open-ended.*

The Other Side of Places

The word "landscape" as it has been used in Western art history refers generally to nature that has been subjected to the artificial influences of humankind. In his book on landscapes, François Jullien writes that if the formation of landscape incorporates the world as a whole, that place becomes a whole in itself, creating endless interactions and communication.[12] This section on "The Other Side of Places" goes even farther by recalling the dictionary definition of place as "a setting in which something occurs or that performs some role." In particular, it shares works of art that incorporate reflections on the near future, history, and the present-day contradictions taking place on the other side of a landscape reflecting a particular place.

Using photography and video to understand and approach different cultures, Han Sungpil speaks to the epistemological chaos that results from the confusion of illusion and fiction, reality and representation, falsehood and truth. This exhibition includes three works from the artist's *Ground Cloud* series (2005/2012). The striking feature of this work is the white smoke that cuts through the blue sky within this seemingly peaceful and bucolic landscape — in fact, the work is a landscape of one of the largest nuclear power plants in France, located at Nogent-sur-Seine. The steam that emerges from the large smokestack and spreads over the clear sky and field in this peaceful farming village creates a peculiar image combining a sense of peace and terror with a nuclear power plant — one of the most representative examples of a convenience of modern civilization. The landscape illustrates the differences and boundaries between the emotional responses that emerge as we confront the ideal understanding and reality of nuclear power through the transformation into a "real but surreal *mise-en-scène*."

Laurent Grasso seeks to adopt a new perspective on history and reality by using media such as drawing, painting, installation, sculpture, and video to visualize the various invisible forces that affect human perception — including multilayered temporality, supernatural phenomena, and collective fear. Surveying the visible world through invisible things, Grasso identifies certain commonalities. They are depicted from a scientific perspective, a cosmic perspective that transcends science, or from a multidimensional perspective that seems to permit travel from past to future or from future to past. *The Silent Movie* (2010) is a work presented by the artist at the eighth edition of Manifesta. Filmed in a coastal military region in Cartagena, Spain, the video work shows a sea and the seemingly peaceful coastal landscape that surrounds it, before going to present images that gradually reveal the camouflaged military facilities in the vicinity. While the images appear to show a peaceful and attractive coastal scene, the presence of the military facilities in a landscape without personae attest to the present and the traces left behind by history. A black submarine that periodically appears above the surface of the water alludes to the possibility of a clash occurring in the future. Presenting a scene thick with the tension that hangs over the military coastline, the video illustrates an ambivalent perspective that alternates between the seen and unseen, a perspective of attacking or besieging from a close or distant place, and the external and internal points-of-view. It is considered one of Grasso's representative works, exploring and experimenting the visualize in the artist's language the truth and contradictions that exist on the unseen underside of reality.

MAP Office is a Hong Kong-based artist group consisting of artist Laurent Gutierrez and architect Valérie Portefaix. Through media such as photography, painting, installation, performance, literature, and theoretical texts, they produce work that studies physical and imaginative domains in flexible ways, using their different project to explore the possibilities of different critical perspectives on the Asian region. This exhibition presents the video *Ghost Island* (2019) for the first time since its acquisition by MMCA, along with associated photographs, postcards, and maps. Focusing on the various fishing-related activities that human beings have engaged in on the seas throughout history in order to survive, this ongoing project examines related stories and different cultures from social, economic, and historical perspectives. Conducted as part of an art network spanning different regions of Asian, the work addresses issues of the marine ecosystem, including the sea, corals and other organisms, and garbage such as fishing nets that are discarded or lost in the ocean. *Ghost Island* was produced for exhibition at the inaugural Bangkok Art Biennale in 2017 and combines video with a large, six-meter-tall structure positioned for four months in inter-tidal waters on the coast of Thailand's Krabi region. The use of nets dates back to before the Common Era as people have engaged in fishing as a means of survival throughout history. Produced with synthetic materials since the modern era, nets continued to be used continuously and excessively. While the original purpose of a fishing net is to catch fish, the "ghost nets" that are discarded or lost in the sea function in the opposite way — trapping fish and other organisms within the water and threatening marine ecosystems. The creation of this public project installation involved the collection and upcycling of roughly 300 kilograms of ghost nets, with the collection and recycling of garbage from the surrounding coast resulting in a kind of clean-up project to restore the marine ecosystem. The structure recorded in the *Ghost Island* video assumes a similar shape to islands along the coast — with the artificial island created by the artists altering the coastal topography as it exists among the actual islands. The artwork incorporates multiple layers of meaning and messages regarding a new approach to community in Asian and the restoration of marine ecosystems that are collapsing due to human activities.

Won, Seoungwon is known for her works that form unique narratives mixing reality and imagination through collage techniques that meticulously juxtapose photographic images taken in different times and places. To more deeply explore the realm of the "other" that she attempts to represent, the artist selected six professional job categories in the contemporary era (journalist, IT specialist, professor, pharmacist, financier, government officer, and researcher), encapsulating different perspectives and attitudes toward them within landscapes that painstakingly combine image fragments gathered from actual landscapes. As she explores the different professions, she discovers different hidden aspects within the superficial perspectives toward them. To gather the images symbolizing each of the professional categories, the artist spent two years traveling throughout South Korea and taking thousands of photographs. The numerous high-resolution photographs captured in the process were then subjected to painstaking Photoshop work before re-emerging as imaginary landscapes that exist nowhere on earth. This combination of analog photography methods and labor-intensive photographic collage work by Won exhibits a power and artistry that overwhelm the viewer with both the scale and detail. The sea that appears in *The Sea of Journalists* (2017) is a landscape of enormous waves and typhoon winds, recalling the paintings of J. M. W. Turner in the way they illustrate human helplessness amid the sublime beauty of a vast nature that inspires both fear and splendor. A gap appears to exist between the waves seen by the hyena (journalist) precariously sitting on a boat in the churning waves of the sea and the waves seen by the penguin (also a journalist) standing on a fixed island with a fixed perspective. To capture these vivid images of the sea, Won experienced three typhoons, risking her life to track the course of their winds. Amassed and recombined, the different waves encompass different times and places simultaneously.

The Water-grass Network of IT Specialists (2017) uses its landscape to represent IT specialists seeking and creating new value amid the data and countless networks that exist in the virtual realm. The artist uses the thick patches of water-grass that grow by a river to represent the flows of invisible online data. The movement of the grass with the current incorporates and visualizes the information of the unseen water deeper down. As the amount of water increases, the plants form enormous flows according to the speed and direction of the water — an image that mirrors the flows of culture and trends online. The birds of different species resemble IT specialists searching intently through the vast flows of the water-grass to identify what is present there.

1 François Jullien, *Living Off Landscape*, Rowman & Littlefield, London, 2018, p. 3.
2 Ma Sun-ja, *Nature, Landscape, and the Human Being*, Acanet, Paju, 2003, p. 56.
3 Jullien, op. cit., p. 5.
4 Alison Butler et al. (eds.), *Eija-Liisa Ahtila: Parallel worlds*, Steidl, Göttingen, 2012, p. 23.
5 The "G" in the territory's name is a reference to Gondwana, a supercontinent that once encompassed all of the land in the current Southern Hemisphere.
6 Sejin Kim's artist notes.
7 Ma, op. cit., p. 279. The author writes, "As the symptoms of late industrial society began emerging during this time period, it was an obvious consequence that the natural environment would become increasingly important to artists and emerge as a new focus of attention. If we consider how landscapes have always been an important source of inspiration for humankind and for Western artists, the search for new possibilities in nature and the environment by artists frustrated with the languages of technology, consumer culture, and art-for-art's-sake could be seen an avant-garde tradition among artists, who tend to be ahead of the curve in reading the zeitgeist." It is this kind of ecological artists' group in which David Nash served as an important member.
8 Andrew Lambith & David Nash, *David Nash*, Kukje Gallery, Seoul, 2007, p. 31.
9 Ma, op. cit., p. 82: "Poussin's The *Four Seasons* emerged out of a tradition of calendar paintings representing solar terms. But Poussin did not confine himself to conveying the sense of natural changes and customs with the changing of the seasons. His four seasons symbolize the four times of the day, as well as the journey of life. His representations of the freshness of the morning when the sun rises, the brightness of the sun at midday, the richness of the afternoon hours, and the darkening of twilight are depictions not simply of the four seasons but of the four times of day, and at the same time symbols of the journey of life from birth to death. In this set of paintings, Poussin sought to precisely render the broad spectrum of color tones associated with changes in nature and the subtle states of light."
10 Jeffrey Kastner (Ed.), *Nature*, Whitechapel Gallery; The MIT Press, London; Cambridge, MA, 2012, p. 28.
11 E.A.T (Experiments in Art and Technology) founded in New York in 1966 is a pioneering non-profit group that began actively promoting and exploring the union of art and technology.
12 Jullien, op. cit., p. 244.

1.
THE WHOLE
OF PARTS

부분의 전체

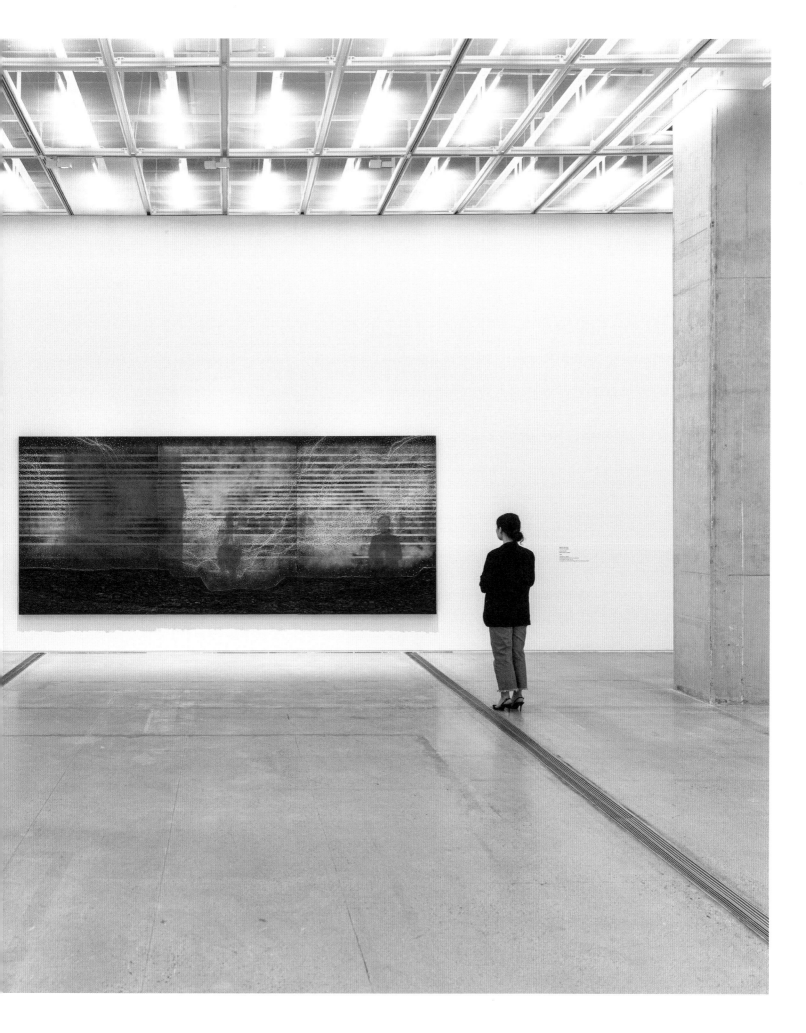

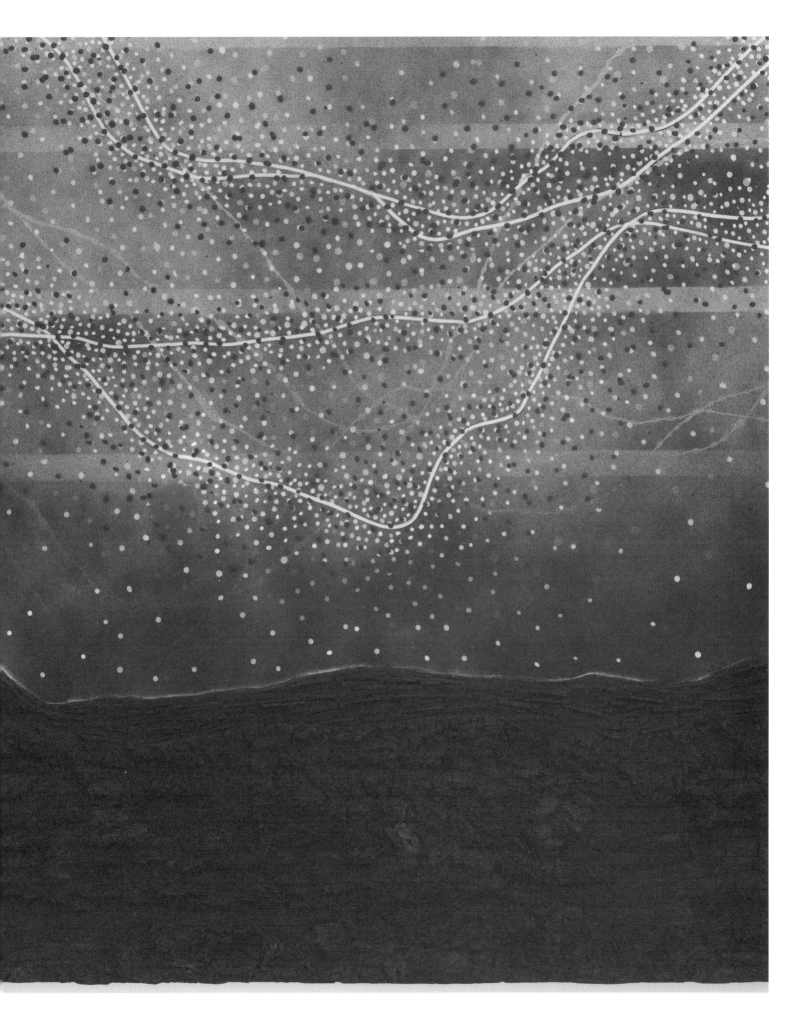

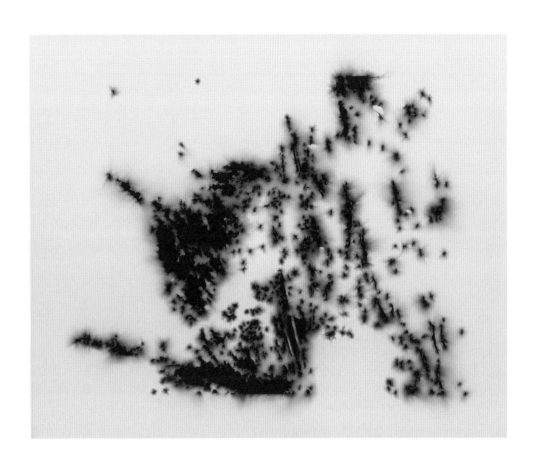

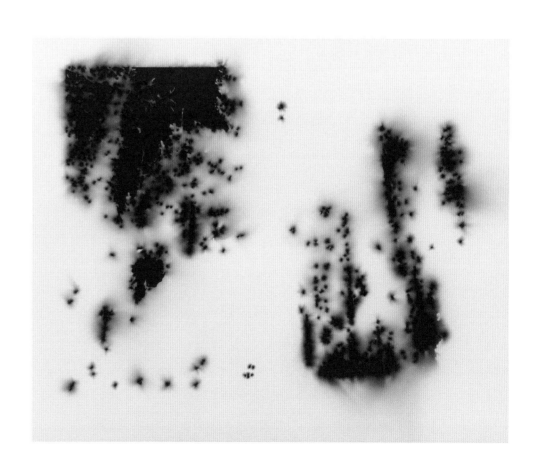

Daylight savings time ended this morning. Always a weird moment for me because I hate the darkness of winter. Don't know ___ was on the radio today, and I found his story inspiring. Makes me want to go to NY Noodletown to try their ginger scallion noodles.

11/1/09   4 pm
232 3rd St., Brooklyn

We had a nice birthday party for Dad last night. We wanted
to go to the jacuzzi after, but it was storming. This morning is
clear but cold. We're heading back to N.Y.C. Glenn got a
great write up in the Times for the Whitney show. I'm
not sure I'm ready for the city, but life moves on.

2/27/11 7:00 a.m.
La Jolla

We are on our way to Yale for Emmett's graduation. So proud of him!
Mom and Dad are here for another week then off to Europe with Emmett
and Ella. Lisa and Ella were helpful about alleviating my anxiety
over the show. It'll be what it is.

5/17/15   8 a.m.
Gowanus

2.
THE VOLUME
OF PHENOMENA

현상의 부피

AXIS OF HORIZON

수평의 축

2020. 4. 6 – 5. 17. Gallery 2
2020. 4. 17 – 5. 17. Gallery 3, 4

〈수평의 축〉전은 국립현대미술관의 국제미술 소장품을 중심으로 구성된 기획전시이다. 이 전시는 르네상스 이후 근대로 이행하면서 오랫동안 탐색되고 예술의 재현을 시도해 온 전통적인 소재이자 주제인 '자연'을 동시대적 관점에서 재해석하고 다양한 형태로 조명하고자 기획되었다.

서양 미술사에서 '자연'은 종교와 인간중심의 사고(틀)에서 파생된 주제인 신화, 종교, 역사, 초상에 가려져 17세기에 이르러서야 풍경화라는 독자적인 장르가 확립되면서 미술에서 적극적으로 다뤄지게 되었다. 〈수평의 축〉전은 자연을 표로로 주체적인 미술의 대상으로 삼았던 풍경화를 이후 지속적으로 변화해 온 자연에 대한 접근방식을 보여준다. 이것은 현대미술의 미학적인 실험을 거쳐 생성되는 재해석을 바탕으로 한 자연에 대한 탐구뿐만 아니라 자연과 인간의 관계, 사회와 개인 그리고 역사를 포괄적으로 다룬다. 또한 조각, 사진, 영상, 설치 등 다양한 시각예술 장르로 실험되고 확장되는 작품들은 다차원적인 관점에서 다층적인 의미를 내포한다.

전통적으로 동양적 자연관이 사람의 인위적인 힘이 가해지지 않은 상태의 자연을 의미한다면, 서양의 자연관은 자연을 하나의 정복의 대상으로 연구했다. 우리가 일반적으로 말하는 '풍경' 또한 자연을 개척하거나 다양한 형식의 문명적 상태로 변환한 풍경을 의미한다. 원초적이며 이상적 자연을 의미하는 아르카디아(Arcadia)라는 개념이 서양의 오랜 역사에 존재하지만, 그것 역시 인간에 이상(理想)을 중심에 둔 자연관에서 생겨난 아름답고, 풍요로운 유토피아일 뿐이다. 여기서 살펴보고자 하는 자연은 보이는 것들의 이면에 존재하는 현재와 역사, 개인과 사회, 자연의 현상 자체가 하나의 작품으로 응축되고 변환되는 넓은 의미의 자연을 말한다. '수평의 축'이라는 전시 제목은 하늘이 대지 혹은 수면과 맞닿는 수평의 접점에서 다양한 좌표를 그려볼 수 있는 축(axis) 세우기를 시도함으로서 자연의 내부와 외부, 인간과 문명의 경계를 우연하게 넘나드는 새로운 관점을 제시해 보고자 하는 의미를 함축한다. 그런 의미에서 자연은 다른 세계와 차원을 바라보게 하는 창이자 문지방(threshold)과 같은 경계에 존재하는 것으로 시간, 역사, 인간, 그리고 자연 스스로 존재해 온 방식 속에서 형성된 길항관계를 보여준다. 더하여 이번 전시는 자연에 대한 묘사와 재현, 삶에 대한 사유, 그리고 인간이 자연의 일부라는 자각을 일깨우면서 등 대의 미술이 함의하는 메시지들을 통해 현재에 대한 반성과 미래에 대한 모색을 꾀한다.

Axis of Horizon is a feature exhibition focusing on work from the international art collection of the National Museum of Modern and Contemporary Art, Korea (MMCA). The exhibition was designed to show contemporary reinterpretations of "nature"–a traditional subject matter and theme that has long been explored and used as a focus of artistic representation in the post-Renaissance transition to modernity–and to explore it in different forms.

In the history of Western art, "nature" was long overshadowed by mythology, religion, history, and portraiture as themes derived from religion and human-centered thinking; it was not until the 17th century that landscapes became established as an independent genre that was actively pursued in art. Axis of Horizon illustrates approaches toward nature that have undergone continuous transformations since the first landscape paintings that regarded nature as a topic for subjective artistic treatment. In addition to exploring nature based on its reinterpretations through aesthetic experimentation within contemporary art, the exhibition takes a comprehensive look at the relationship between nature and human beings, society and the individual, and history. Works of art that show experimentation with and expansion into a range of different visual arts genres–including sculpture, photography, the moving image, and installations–also encompass multiple layers of meaning from a multi-dimensional perspective.

If the Eastern view of nature is understood to signify nature that has not been subjected to artificial human forces, then the view of nature in the West has treated it as a subject of conquest. The concept of the "landscape" as we ordinarily use it also refers to nature that has been developed or natural scenes that have been transformed into different forms of civilized states. The concept of "Arcadia" as an ideal, primeval form of nature has long existed in Western history, but even this is but a beautiful and abundant utopia that originates a view of nature centering on human ideals. The nature that is to be examined here is nature in a broader sense, where the elements that exist behind what is seen–the present time and history, the individual and society, the phenomena of nature themselves– are condensed and transformed into individual artistic works. The exhibition title "Axis of Horizon" symbolizes the aim of presenting a new perspective–one that freely crosses boundaries between within and outside of nature, or between humanity and civilization–by attempting to establish an "axis" for portraying different coordinates along the horizontal point of contact where sky meets earth or water. In that sense, nature is something that exists on the boundaries, like a window or threshold looking into different worlds and dimensions, illustrating the competitive relationships that have formed within the ways in which time, history, humanity, and nature itself have existed. Through its depictions and representations of nature, contemplations of life, and the messages implicit in contemporary art as it evokes an awareness of humanity as part of nature, the exhibition aspires to reflect on the present while exploring the future.

3.
THE OTHER SIDE OF PLACES

장소의 이면

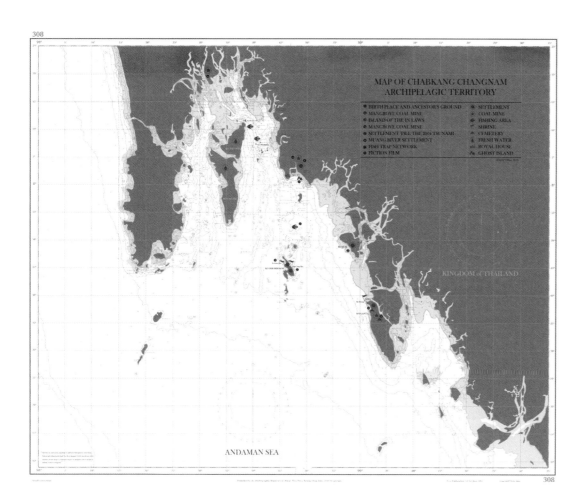

MAP OF CHABKANG CHANGNAM
ARCHIPELAGIC TERRITORY

- BIRTH PLACE AND ANCESTOR'S GROUND
- MANGROVE COAL MINE
- ISLAND OF THE IN LAWS
- MANGROVE COAL MINE
- SETTLEMENT TILL THE 2004 TSUNAMI
- MUANG RIVER SETTLEMENT
- FISH TRAP NETWORK
- FICTION FILM

- SETTLEMENT
- COAL MINE
- FISHING AREA
- SHRINE
- CEMETERY
- FRESH WATER
- ROYAL HOUSE
- GHOST ISLAND

KINGDOM of THAILAND

ANDAMAN SEA

작품 목록 List of Artworks

19 토마스 스트루스, 〈파라다이스 21, 주케이, 브라질 2001〉, 크로모제닉 프린트, 180.1×223.8cm, 2001. 국립현대미술관 소장.
Thomas Struth, *Paradise 21, Yuquehy, Brazil 2001*, Chromogenic print, 180.1×223.8cm, 2001. MMCA Collection. © Thomas Struth

20 에이샤-리사 아틸라, 〈수평-바카수오라〉, 6채널 비디오, 컬러, 사운드, 6분 3초, 2011. 국립현대미술관 발전 후원 위원회 기증. 국립현대미술관 소장.
Eija-Liisa Ahtila, *Horizontal-Vaakasuora*, Six-channel video, color, sound, 6min. 3sec., 2011. Donated to MMCA Director's Council (MDC). MMCA Collection.

24 테레시타 페르난데즈, 〈은빛 하늘〉, 나무판넬에 고체흑연, 연필, 91.4×121.9×5.1cm, 2016. 작가 및 리만머핀 뉴욕, 홍콩, 서울 제공.
Teresita Fernández, *Nocturnal (Silver Sky)*, Solid graphite and pencil on wood panel, 91.4×121.9×5.1cm, 2016. Courtesy the Artist and Lehmann Maupin, New York, Hong Kong, and Seoul.

26 테레시타 페르난데즈, 〈어두운 땅(우주)〉, 크롬판넬에 목탄, 혼합매체, 203.2×487.7×5.1cm, 2019. 사진: 엘리자베스 번스타인. 작가 및 리만머핀 뉴욕, 홍콩, 서울 제공.
Teresita Fernández, *Dark Earth (Cosmos)*, Solid charcoal and mixed media on chromed panel, 203.2×487.7×5.1cm, 2019. Photo: Elisabeth Bernstein. Courtesy the Artist and Lehmann Maupin, New York, Hong Kong, and Seoul.

30 테레시타 페르난데즈, 〈비냘레스(자궁)〉, 나무판넬에 혼합매체, 각 15.2×20.3×5.1cm(8판넬), 2015. 사진: 엘리자베스 번스타인. 작가 및 리만머핀 뉴욕, 홍콩, 서울 제공.
Teresita Fernández, *Viñales (Cervix)*, Mixed media on wood panel, each 15.2×20.3×5.1cm (8 panels), 2015. Photo: Elisabeth Bernstein. Courtesy the Artist and Lehmann Maupin, New York, Hong Kong, and Seoul.

32 테레시타 페르난데즈, 〈타버린 풍경(아메리카) 1〉, 불에 태운 레이저 컷 종이, 각 40×47.6×4.4cm(8개), 2017. 작가 및 리만머핀 뉴욕, 홍콩, 서울 제공.
Teresita Fernández, *Burned Landscape (America) I*, Burned, laser-cut paper, each 40×47.6×4.4cm (8 parts), 2017. Courtesy the Artist and Lehmann Maupin, New York, Hong Kong, and Seoul.

38 데이비드 내시, 〈줄무늬의 달리는 사람〉, 나무, 193×132×110cm, 1989. 국립현대미술관 소장.
David Nash, *Striped Runner*, Wood, 193×132×110cm, 1989. MMCA Collection. © David Nash / DACS, London - SACK, Seoul, 2020.

40 김세진, 〈2048〉, 단채널 HD 비디오, 스테레오 사운드, 31분 18초, 2020. 작가 소장.
Sejin Kim, *2048*, Single-channel video, stereo sound, 31min. 18sec., 2020. Courtesy the Artist. © sejinkimstudio

44 제니퍼 스타인캠프, 〈정물 3〉, 영상 설치, 가변크기, 2019. 작가 및 리만머핀 뉴욕, 홍콩, 서울 제공.
Jennifer Steinkamp, *Still-life 3*, Video installation, Dimensions variable, 2019. Courtesy the Artist and Lehmann Maupin, New York, Hong Kong, and Seoul.

48 바이런 킴, 〈일요일 회화 11/2/09〉, 캔버스에 아크릴릭, 펜, 35.5×35.5×3.2cm, 2009. 사진: 박준형. 작가 소장, 국제갤러리 제공.
Byron Kim, *Sunday Painting 11/2/09*, Acrylic and pen on canvas, 35.5×35.5×3.2cm, 2009. Photo: Keith Park. Courtesy the Artist and Kukje Gallery.

49 바이런 킴, 〈일요일 회화 2/27/11〉, 캔버스에 아크릴릭, 펜, 35.5×35.5×3.2cm, 2011. 사진: 박준형. 작가 소장, 국제갤러리 제공.
Byron Kim, *Sunday Painting 2/27/11*, Acrylic and pen on canvas, 35.5×35.5×3.2cm, 2011. Photo: Keith Park. Courtesy the Artist and Kukje Gallery.

54 바이런 킴, 〈일요일 회화 5/17/15〉, 캔버스에 아크릴릭, 펜, 35.5×35.5×3.2cm, 2015. 사진: 박준형. 작가 소장, 국제갤러리 제공.
Byron Kim, *Sunday Painting 5/17/15*, Acrylic and pen on canvas, 35.5×35.5×3.2cm, 2015. Photo: Keith Park. Courtesy the Artist and Kukje Gallery.

57 올라퍼 엘리아슨, 〈사각 구체〉, 스테인리스 스틸 거울, 황동, 지름 90cm, 2007. 삼성미술관 Leeum.
Olafur Eliasson, *Square Sphere*, Stainless steel mirrors, bronzed brass, Diameter 90cm, 2007 Leeum, Samsung Museum of Art.

58 팀 프렌티스, 〈부드러운 비〉, 153개의 알루미늄 막대, 100×870×390cm, 2002. 국립현대미술관 소장.
Tim Prentice, *Soft Rain*, 153 Aluminum rods, 100×870×390cm, 2002. MMCA Collection.

60 헤수스 라파엘 소토, 〈파고들다〉, 비닐호스, 아크릴판, 조명등, 330×480×440cm, 1988. 국립현대미술관 소장.
Jesús Rafael Soto, *Penetrable*, Vinyle-wire, acrylic plate, light, 330×480×440cm, 1988. MMCA Collection. © Jesús Rafael Soto / ADAGP, Paris - SACK, Seoul, 2020.

62 앤디 골즈워시, 〈무제(백)〉, 종이에 크레용, 오일스틱, 170×148cm, 1989. 국립현대미술관 소장.
Andy Goldsworthy, *Untitled(White)*, Crayon, oilstick on paper, 170×148cm, 1989. MMCA Collection.

63 앤디 골즈워시, 〈무제(흑)〉, 종이에 크레용, 오일스틱, 158×146cm, 1989. 국립현대미술관 소장.
Andy Goldsworthy, *Untitled(Black)*, Crayon, oilstick on paper, 158×146cm, 1989. MMCA Collection.

65 한스 하케, 〈아이스 테이블〉, 스테인리스 스틸, 냉동장치, 91.4×92×49cm, 1967. 국립현대미술관 소장.
Hans Haacke, *Ice Table*, Stainless steel, refrigeration unit, 91.4×92×49cm, 1967. MMCA Collection.

66 박기원, 〈넓이〉, 장지에 유채, 214×150cm, 2007-2008. 국립현대미술관 소장.
Kiwon Park, *Width*, Oil on *jangji* paper, 214×150cm, 2007-2008. MMCA Collection.

73 한성필, 〈그라운드 클라우드 034〉, 아카이벌 피그먼트 프린트, 121×162cm, 2005/2012. 국립현대미술관 소장.
Han Sungpil, *Ground Cloud 034*, Archival pigment print, 121×162cm, 2005/2012. MMCA Collection.

75 한성필, 〈그라운드 클라우드 026〉, 아카이벌 피그먼트 프린트, 121×162cm, 2005/2012. 국립현대미술관 소장.
Han Sungpil, *Ground Cloud 026*, Archival pigment print, 121×162cm, 2005/2012. MMCA Collection.

76 원성원, 〈언론인의 바다〉, C-프린트, 178×297cm, 2017. 국립현대미술관 소장.
Won, Seoungwon, *The Sea of Journalists*, C-print, 178×297cm, 2017. MMCA Collection.

78 원성원, 〈IT 전문가의 물-풀 네트워크〉, C-프린트, 178×297cm, 2017. 국립현대미술관 소장.
Won, Seoungwon, *The Water-grass Network of IT specialists*, C-print, 178×297cm, 2017. MMCA Collection.

80 맵 오피스, 〈유령 섬〉, 피그먼트 프린트, 각 160×90cm, 2018. 작가 소장.
MAP Office, *Ghost Island*, Pigment prints, each 160×90cm, 2018. Courtesy the Artist.

82 맵 오피스, 〈유령 섬〉, 엽서, 해양지도, 2018. 작가 소장.
MAP Office, *Ghost Island*, Postcard series, nautical map, 2018. Courtesy the Artist.

83 맵 오피스, 〈유령 섬〉, HD 비디오, 사운드, 38분, 2019. 국립현대미술관 소장.
MAP Office, *Ghost Island*, HD video, sound, 38min., 2019. MMCA Collection.

84 로랑 그라소, 〈무성영화〉, 단채널 비디오, 컬러, 사운드, 23분 27초, 2010. 국립현대미술관 소장.
Laurent Grasso, *The Silent Movie*, Single-channel video, color, sound, 23min. 27sec., 2010. MMCA Collection.

에이샤-리사 아틸라

에이샤-리사 아틸라(b.1959, 핀란드)는 헬싱키대학교에서 법학과를 졸업한 후, 런던 컬리지 오브 프린팅, 미국 영화연구소, 캘리포니아대학교에서 영화와 비디오를 공부했다. 작가는 최근 호주 무빙-이미지센터(2017, 멜버른), 구겐하임 미술관(2016, 빌바오), 이스라엘미술관(2014, 예루살렘) 등에서 개인전을 개최했으며, 웨일즈 국제 시각예술상(2006), 스웨덴 유진 황태자 우수예술훈장(2009) 등을 수여 받았다.

토마스 스트루스

토마스 스트루스(b.1954, 독일)는 독일 쿤스트아카데미 뒤셀도르프에서 회화와 사진을 전공했으며, 최근 폴크바그 미술관(2016, 에센), 마틴-그로피우스-바우(2016, 베를린), 하이 미술관(2017, 아틀랜타), 무디아트센터(2017, 휴스턴), 하우스 데르 쿤스트(2018, 뮌헨), 구겐하임 미술관(2019, 빌바오) 등에서 개인전을 개최했다. 9회 도큐멘타(1992), 베니스건축비엔날레(2012) 등 국제전에 참여했으며, 베르너 만츠 사진상(1992), 니더작센재단 국제스펙트럼 사진상(1997)을 수상했다.

로랑 그라소

로랑 그라소(b.1972, 프랑스)는 르 크레닥(2004, 이브리-쉬르-센느), 파운데이션 폴 리카르(2006, 파리), 팔래 드 도쿄(2009, 파리), 주 드 폼 국립미술관(2012, 파리), 몬트리올현대미술관(2013), 션 켈리 갤러리(2019, 뉴욕) 등에서 다수의 개인전을 개최했으며, 마르셀 뒤샹(2008)상과 예술문학훈장(2015)을 수여 받았다.

헤수스 라파엘 소토

옵 아트와 키네틱 아트의 대가 헤수스 라파엘 소토(1923-2005, 베네수엘라)는 카라카스 예술학교에서 수학한 후, 1950년에 파리로 활동지를 옮겨 일생을 보냈다. 1949년부터 개최해온 수많은 개인전 중 대표적인 것으로는 시카고현대미술관(1971), 구겐하임 미술관(1974, 뉴욕), 파리현대미술관(1979) 등이 있고, 최근에는 퐁피두센터(2013, 파리), 휴스턴미술관(2014), 에스파스 루이비통(2019, 도쿄) 등의 미술관에서 회고전이 개최되었다.

팀 프렌티스

팀 프렌티스(b.1930, 미국)는 예일대에서 건축을 전공한 후 건축가로 활동하다가 40대의 나이에 조금 늦게 조각을 시작했다. 그럼에도 1976년에 AT&T 롱라인과의 첫 커미션 작업을 시작으로 어빙아트센터(1991), 맥코믹전시관(1997, 시카고), 국립현대미술관(2002, 과천) 등과 함께 왕성하게 협업해왔다. 그는 미술기관뿐만 아니라 파에노과학센터(2014, 볼프스부르그), 딕시 응용기술대학 (2017, 세인트 조지), 도미니언 에너지(2019, 리치몬드) 등과 같은 과학기술기관과의 커미션 작업을 통해 특유의 건축적이면서도 기발한 예술세계를 드러내며 키네틱 아트의 거장으로 평가받고 있다.

데이비드 내시

데이비드 내시(b.1945, 영국)는 킹스턴 예술대학에서 수학한 후 첼시 예술대학에서 대학원 과정을 마쳤다. 1973년에 열린 첫 개인전 이후 다수의 개인전을 개최했으며, 영국 요크셔 조각공원(2010), 큐 왕립식물원(2012-13, 리치먼드)과 샤또 쇼몽-쉬르-루아르(2013, 프랑스)에서 개최된 전시가 대표적이다. 그의 작품은 런던 테이트 모던, 빅토리아 앤 알버트 미술관과 뉴욕 메트로폴리탄미술관, 구겐하임 미술관 등 유명 기관에 소장되어 있으며, 2004년에는 예술계에 대한 공로를 인정받아 대영제국 4등 훈장을 수훈하였다.

앤디 골즈워시

앤디 골즈워시(b.1956, 영국)는 브래드포드 예술대학과 프레스턴 과학·기술 전문학교에서 예술을 전공한 후, 1980년부터 활발히 활동하고 있는데 주요 개인전으로는 요크셔 조각 공원(2007), 네드 스미스 자연·예술센터(2010, 펜실베니아), 데코르도바 조각 공원·미술관(2001, 매사추세츠) 등에서 개최한 전시가 있다. 요크셔 예술상(1980), 노던 아트 어워드(1981-1982), 스코틀랜드 예술위원상(1987)을 수상하기도 했다.

박기원

박기원(b.1964, 한국)은 작가는 국립충북대학교에서 서양화를 전공하고, 멜버른현대사진센터(1997), 아르코미술관(2006, 서울), 레이나 소피아 국립아트센터(2006, 마드리드), 국립현대미술관(2010, 과천), 그랑 팔래(2016, 파리) 등의 미술관에서 다수의 개인전을 개최했다. 2010년에는 국립현대미술관의 올해의 작가로 선정되었으며, 13회 중앙뉴스 문화예술상을 수상했다.

한스 하케

한스 하케(b.1936, 독일)는 카셀 주립예술아카데미에서 순수예술 석사과정에 준하는 국가고시 자격증을 취득한 후, 템플대학교 타일러 순수예술학교를 졸업했다. 대표적인 개인전으로는 안토니오 라티 재단(2010, 코모), MIT 리스트 비주얼 아트 센터(2011, 매사추세츠), 레이나 소피아 국립아트센터(2012, 마드리드)에서 열린 전시가 있으며, 베니스비엔날레에서 황금사자상(1993)과 페터바이스상(2004)을 수상했다.

원성원

원성원(b.1972, 한국)은 중앙대학교 조소과를 졸업하고, 쿤스트아카데미 뒤셀도르프에서 마이스터슐러, 쾰른 미디어 예술대학에서 석사 학위를 받았다. 2001년 본 미술협회에서 첫 개인전을 개최한 이후, IP 도이치랜드(2002, 쾰른), 갤러리 가나-보부르그(2005, 파리), 대안공간 루프(2008, 서울), 가나 컨템포러리(2010, 서울) 등에서 개인전을 선보였다.

한성필

한성필(b.1972, 한국)은 중앙대학교 사진학과와 킹스턴대학교 대학원 큐레이팅 컨템포러리 디자인 석사과정을 마쳤다. 주요 개인전으로는 인데코갤러리(1999, 서울), 휴스턴 포토페스트 헤드쿼터스 갤러리(2004, 텍사스), 라이트 컨템포러리(2005, 런던), 아라리오갤러리(2011, 서울), 라틴아메리카 한국문화원(2014, 부에노스 아이레스) 등에서 개최한 전시가 있다.

테레시타 페르난데즈

개념예술가 테레시타 페르난데즈(b.1968, 미국)는 플로리다국제대학교와 버지니아 커먼웰스대학교에서 예술을 전공했으며, 말랑가현대예술센터(2005), 클리블랜드현대미술관(2011), 매사추세츠현대미술관(2014), 마이애미 페레즈미술관(2019), 포에닉스미술관(2020) 등 해외 주요 미술관에서 개인전을 개최했다. 루이스 컴포트 티파니 비엔날레상(1999), 구겐하임 펠로우쉽(2003), 맥아더 재단 펠로우쉽(2005), 아스펜 예술상(2013)을 수여 받았으며, 2017년에는 국립 뮤지엄·스쿨 학술위원으로 선출되었다.

제니퍼 스타인캠프

제니퍼 스타인캠프(b.1958, 미국)는 패서디나 디자인예술대학에서 석사과정까지 마쳤으며, 주요 개인전으로는 산호세현대미술관(2006), 말랑가현대예술센터(2009), 휴스턴미술관(2012, 2014), 샌디에고현대미술관(2011, 2016), 클라크 아트인스티튜트(2018, 윌리엄스타운) 등에서 개최된 전시가 있다. 이외에도 카이로국제비엔날레(2008), 이스탄불비엔날레(2003) 등 다수의 국제전에 참여했다.

바이런 킴

한국계 미국 작가 바이런 킴(b.1961, 미국)은 주변 지인들의 다양한 피부색을 394개의 패널에 그린 대형설치작품 〈제유법〉을 휘트니비엔날레(1993)에 출품하면서 세계적인 주목을 받기 시작했다. 작가는 예일대 영문학과와 스코히건 회화조각학교를 졸업했으며, 주요 개인전으로는 AC 프로젝트룸(1992, 뉴욕), 휘트니미술관(1999, 뉴욕), 제임스 코한 갤러리(2011, 뉴욕),

샌디에고현대미술관(2015), 클리블랜드현대미술관(2019) 등에서 개최된 전시가 있다. 그는 미국예술문학회 예술부문 루이스 네벨슨상(1993)과 로버트 드니로 상(2019)을 비롯한 다수의 상과 기금을 수여 받기도 했다.

올라퍼 엘리아슨

올라퍼 엘리아슨(b.1967, 덴마크)은 덴마크왕립미술학교를 졸업한 후, 1995년에 스튜디오를 설립하여 공예, 건축, 프로그래머, 테크니션 등 각 분야의 전문가들과 협업하고 있다. 2003년 베니스 비엔날레와 테이트 모던의 날씨 프로젝트를 통해 국제적으로 주목받기 시작했으며, 샌프란시스코현대미술관(2007), 뉴욕현대미술관(2010), 루이비통 재단 미술관(2015, 파리), 삼성미술관리움(2016, 서울) 등 세계 유수의 미술관에서 개인전을 개최했다.

맵 오피스

로랑 구티에레즈와 발레리 폭트패로 구성된 작가 그룹 맵 오피스(est.1996, 홍콩)는 실제적 혹은 상상적 영토를 드로잉, 사진, 비디오, 설치, 퍼포먼스 등 다양한 조형언어로 표현한다. 주요 개인전으로는 파라/사이트 아트센터(2004, 홍콩), 괴테 인스티튜트(2008, 홍콩), 아시아 아트 아카이브(2012, 홍콩), 상하이아트갤러리(2013), 디아 프로젝트(2015, 호치민)에서 개최한 전시가 있으며, 베니스건축비엔날레(2000), 이스탄불비엔날레(2007), 광주비엔날레(2008), 아시아퍼시픽트리엔날레(2012), 태국비엔날레(2018) 등 다수의 국제전에 참여했다.

Eija-Liisa Ahtila

Born in Finland in 1959, Eija-Liisa Ahtila graduated in law from the University of Helsinki before going on to study cinema and video at the London College of Printing, the American Film Institute, and the University of California, LA. In recent years, she has held solo exhibitions at the Australian Centre for the Moving Image (2017, Melbourne), the Solomon R. Guggenheim Museum in Bilbao (2016), and the Israel Museums (2014, Jerusalem). She has been awarded the Wales International Visual Arts Prize (2006) and Sweden's Prince Eugen Medal for Outstanding Artistic Achievement (2009), among other honors.

Thomas Struth

Born in Germany in 1954, Thomas Struth studied painting and photography at the Kunstakademie Düsseldorf. Recently, he has held solo exhibitions at the Museum Folkwang (2016, Essen), Martin-Gropius-Bau (2016, Berlin), the High Museum of Art (2017, Atlanta), the Moody Center for the Arts (2017, Houston), the Haus der Kunst (2018, Munich), and the Guggenheim Museum in Bilbao (2019). He has taken part in such international events as the 9th Documenta exhibition (1992) and Venice Architecture Biennale (2015), and he has been awarded the Werner Mantz Prize for Photography (1992) and the Spectrum-International Prize for Photographer of the Foundation of Lower Saxony (1997).

Laurent Grasso

Born in 1972 in France, Laurent Grasso has held numerous solo exhibitions at institutions such as Le Crédac (2004, Ivry-sur-Seine), the Fondation Paul Ricard (2016, Paris), the Palais de Tokyo (2009, Paris), Jeu de Paume (2012, Paris), the Musée d'Art Contemporain de Montréal (2013), and Sean Kelly Gallery (2019, New York City). He has been awarded the Prix Marcel Duchamp (2008) and the Chevalier de l'Ordre des Arts et des Lettres (2015).

Jesús Rafael Soto

A master of optical art and kinetic art, Venezuelan artist Jesús Rafael Soto (1923–2005) studied at the Plastic and Applied Arts School in Caracas before moving in 1950 to Paris, which would remain his artistic base for the rest of his life. The most prominent of his numerous solo exhibitions since 1949 include those held at the Museum of Contemporary Art Chicago (1971), the Guggenheim Museum in New York (1974), and the Musée National d'Art Moderne, Paris (1979). Recent retrospectives have been held at the Centre Pompidou (2013, Paris), the Museum of Fine Arts, Houston (2014), and the Espace Louis Vuitton (2019, Tokyo).

Tim Prentice

Born in the US in 1930, Tim Prentice majored in architecture at Yale University and practiced as an architect before beginning his sculpting career at a relatively late age in his forties. His first commissioned work with AT&T Long Lines in 1976 would mark the start of prolific collaborations with the Irving Art Center (1991), the McCormick Exhibition Facility (1997, Chicago), and the National Museum of Modern and Contemporary Art, Korea (2002, Gwacheon). Seen as a master of kinetic art, he has shared his unique artistic vision — at once architectural, offbeat, and novel — through commissioned works not only for art institutions, but also for institutions of science and technology such as the Phaeno Science Center (2014, Wolfsburg), the Dixie Applied Technology College (2017, St. George), and Dominion Energy (2019, Richmond).

David Nash

Born in 1945 in the United Kingdom, David Nash studied at the Kingston College of Art before completing a postgraduate program at the Chelsea School of Art. He has held numerous solo exhibitions since his first in 1973, with some of the most notable taking place at Yorkshire Sculpture Park (2010), Kew Royal Botanic Gardens (2012–13, Richmond), and the Château Chaumont-sur-Loire (2013, France). His works has been added to collections of such noted institutions as London's Tate Gallery and Victoria and Albert Museum and New York City's Metropolitan Museum of Art and Guggenheim Museum. In 2004, he was presented with an Order of the British Empire for service to the arts.

Andy Goldsworthy

Born in 1956 in the United Kingdom, Andy Goldsworthy studied art at the Bradford School of Art and earned a BA from Preston Polytechnic. He has been prolifically active since 1980, with major solo exhibitions held at Yorkshire Sculpture Park (2007), the Ned Smith Center for Nature and Art (2010, Pennsylvania), and deCordova Sculpture Park and Museum (2001, Massachusetts). He has been honored with the Yorkshire Arts Award (1980), the Northern Arts Award (1981–1982), and the Scottish Arts Council Award (1987).

Kiwon Park

Born in South Korea in 1964, Kiwon Park majored in Painting at Chungbuk National university. He has held numerous solo exhibitions at institutions such as the Centre for Contemporary Photography, Melbourne (1997), Arko Art Center (2006, Seoul), the Museo Nacional Centro de Arte Reina Sofia (2006, Madrid), the National Museum of Modern and Contemporary Art, Korea (2010, Gwacheon), and the Grand Palais (2016, Paris). He was selected as Artist of the Year by the National Museum of Modern and Contemporary Art, Korea in 2010, and he has been honored with the 13th Joongang Fine Arts Prize.

Hans Haacke

Born in 1936 in Germany, Hans Haacke received a Staatsexam license (the equivalent of an M.F.A.) from the Staatliche Werkakademie in Kassel and went on to graduate from the Tyler School of Fine Arts at Temple University. His notable solo exhibitions included those held at the Fondazione Antonio Ratti (2010, Como), the MIT List Visual Arts Center (2011, Massachusetts), and the Museo Nacional Centro de Arte Reina Sofia (2012, Madrid). He has been awarded the Venice Biennale's Golden Lion (1993) and the Peter-Weiss-Preis (2004).

Won, Seoungwon

Born in 1972 in South Korea, Won, Seoungwon graduated in sculpture from Chung-Ang University before competing a Meisterschüler program at the Kunstakademie Düsseldorf and a master's degree at the Kunsthochschule für Medien Köln. Since her first solo exhibition in 2001 at the Bonner Kunstverein, she has held solo exhibitions at IP Deutschland (2002, Cologne), Galérie Gana-Beaubourg (2005, Paris), Alternative Space Loop (2008, Seoul), and Gana Contemporary (2010, Seoul).

Han Sungpil

Born in 1972 in South Korea, Han Sungpil studied photography at Chung-Ang University and completing a Curating Contemporary Design graduate program with commendation at Kingston University in London. Among his major solo exhibitions are those held at Gallery Indeco (1999, Seoul), the Houston Fotofest Headquarters gallery (2004, Texas), lightcontemporary (2005, London), Arario Gallery (2011, Seoul), and the Centro Cultural Coreano en América Latina (2014, Buenos Aires).

Teresita Fernández

Born in 1968 in the United States, conceptual artist Teresita Fernández studied at at Florida International University and Virginia Commonwealth University in Richmond. She has held solo exhibitions at such prominent international art institutions as the Centro de Arte Contemporáneo de Málaga (2005), the Museum of Contemporary Art, Cleveland (2011), the Massachusetts Museum of Contemporary Art (2014), the Pérez Art Museum Miami (2019), and Phoenix Art Museum. She has been honored with the Louis Comfort Tiffany Biennial Award (1999), a Guggenheim Fellowship (2003), a MacArthur Foundation Fellowship (2005), and the Aspen Award for Art (2013); in 2017, she was named as a National Academician by the National Academy Museum and School.

Jennifer Steinkamp

Born in 1958 in the United States, Jennifer Steinkamp completed a master's degree at ArtCenter College of Design in Pasadena and has held prominent exhibitions at the San Jose Museum of Contemporary Art (2006), the Centro de Arte Contemporáneo de Málaga (2009), the Museum of Fine Arts Houston (2012 and 2014), the Museum of Contemporary Art, San Diego (2011 and 2016), and the Clark Art Institute (2018, Williamstown). She has also taken part in numerous international exhibition events such as the Cairo International Biennial (2008) and the Istanbul Biennial (2003).

Byron Kim

Born in 1961, the Korean-American artist Byron Kim first rose to global attention in 1993 when his *Synecdoche* — a large installation work featuring the different skin colors of his acquaintances painted on 394 panels — was shown at the Whitney Biennial. A graduate of the English department at Yale University and the Skowhegan School of Painting & Sculpture, the artist has held major solo exhibitions at the AC Project Room (1992, New York City), the Whitney Museum (1999, NYC), the James Cohan Gallery (2011, NYC), the Museum of Contemporary Art, San Diego (2015), and the Museum of Contemporary Art Cleveland (2019). He has received numerous awards and fellowships, including the Louise Nevelson Award in Art from the American Academy of Arts and Letters (1993) and the Robert De Niro, Sr. Prize (2019).

Olafur Eliasson

Born in 1967 in Denmark, Olafur Eliasson graduated from the Royal
Danish Academy of Fine Arts. Since establishing a studio in 1995, he has
collaborated with craftspeople, architects, programmers, technicians, and
other specialists in different fields. He first rose to international attention
through the 2003 Venice Biennale and the Tate Modern's Weather Project.
He has held solo exhibitions at such eminent international art institutions as
the San Francisco Museum of Modern Art (2007), the Museum of Modern
Art (2010, NYC), the Fondation Louis Vuitton (2015, Paris), and Leeum,
Samsung Museum of Art (2016, Seoul).

MAP Office

Established in 1996 in Hong Kong, MAP Office is an artist group consisting
of Laurent Gutierrez and Valérie Portefaix, who represent actual and
imaginary territories in a variety of artistic languages ranging from drawing
to photography, video, installation, and performance. Major solo exhibitions
have been held at Para Site (2004, Hong Kong), the Goethe Institut (2008,
Hong Kong), the Asia Art Archive (2012, Hong Kong), the Shanghai
Gallery of Art (2013), and Dia Projects (2015, Ho Chi Minh City), and
the duo has also taken part in numerous international exhibitions including
the Venice Architecture Biennale (2000), the Istanbul Biennial (2007),
the Gwangju Biennale (2008), the Asia Pacific Triennial (2012), and the
Thailand Biennale (2018).

전시
《수평의 축》

장소
국립현대미술관 서울
2, 3, 4 전시실 및 공용공간

기간
2020. 5. 6. - 2020. 5. 31.

주최
국립현대미술관

총괄
강수정, 박미화

전시 기획
양옥금

전시 진행
정해선

전시 디자인
최유진

그래픽 디자인
강주성, 김유나

설치 · 운영
이길재, 주창하

공간 조성
윤해리

홍보 · 마케팅
윤승연, 박유리
기성미, 신나래
장라윤, 이민지
김홍조, 채지연

교육
정은주, 조정원

고객 지원
이은수, 추헌철, 주다란

보존
범대건, 조인애
남궁훈, 홍진성
권현주, 전상우

사진
김윤재

영상
코코아 픽쳐스

Exhibition
Axis of Horizon

Venue
National Museum of Modern
and Contemporary Art, Seoul
Gallery 2, 3, 4 & Public Space

Period
6 May 2020 – 31 May 2020

Organizer
National Museum of Modern and
Contemporary Art, Korea

Supervisor
Kang Soojung, Park Mihwa

Curator
Okkum Yang

Curatorial Assistant
Haesun Chung

Exhibition Design
Choi Youjin

Graphic Design
Joosung Kang, Kim Yuna

Technical Coordination
Lee Giljae, Ju Changha

Space Construction
Yun Haeri

Public Communication and Marketing
Yun Tiffany, Park Yulee
Ki sungmi, Shin Narae
Jang Layoon, Lee minjee
Kim Hongjo, Chae Jiyeon

Education
Jung Eunjoo, Cho Jeongwon

Customer Support
Lee Eun-su, Chu Hunchul, Ju Daran

Conservation
Beom Daegeon, Cho Inae
Namgung Hun, Hong Jinsung
Kweon HyeonJu, Jeon Sangwoo

Photography
Yoonjae Kim

Film
Cocoa Pictures

출판
이 책은 국립현대미술관에서 개최된
《수평의 축》(2020. 5. 6. - 2020. 5. 31.)
전시 도록으로 제작되었습니다.

발행인
윤범모(국립현대미술관장)

발행처
국립현대미술관
서울시 종로구 삼청로 30
02 3701 9500
www.mmca.go.kr
초판 1쇄 발행 2020. 6.

총괄
양옥금

편집
김은주

도록 디자인
강주성

번역
콜린 모엣

인쇄 · 제책
청산 인쇄

ISBN
978-89-6303-239-9

정가
25,000원

Publication
This book is published as a catalogue
of exhibition, Axis of Horizon, which is
held from 6 May 2020 to 31 May 2020
at the National Museum of Modern and
Contemporary Art, Korea.

Publisher
Youn Bummo (Director, MMCA)

Published by
National Museum of Modern and
Contemporary Art, Korea
30 Samcheong-ro, Jongno-gu,
Seoul, Korea
+82 2 3701 9500
www.mmca.go.kr
First Edition June 2020

Management
Okkum Yang

Editor
Eunju Kim

Design
Joosung Kang

Translation
Colin Mouat

Printing and Binding
Cheongsan Printing

ISBN
978-89-6303-239-9

Price
25,000won

수요일

축